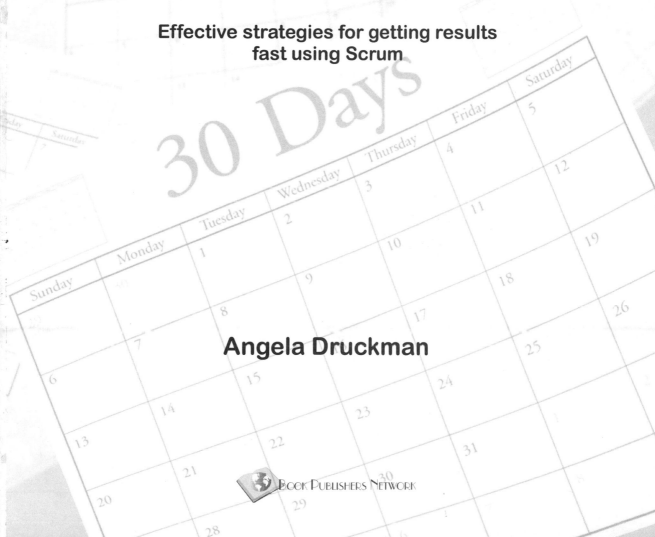

30 Days to Better Agile

Effective strategies for getting results
fast using Scrum

Angela Druckman

BOOK PUBLISHERS NETWORK

Book Publishers Network
P.O. Box 2256
Bothell • WA • 98041
Ph • 425-483-3040
www.bookpublishersnetwork.com

10 9 8 7 6 5 4 3 2 1

Printed in the United States of America

LCCN   2012941435
ISBN   978-1-937454-44-9

Editor: Julie Scandora
Cover Designer: Laura Zugzda
Typographer: Stephanie Martindale

To my rugby team, who always keeps me on my toes.

Contents

Foreword   vii

Acknowledgments   xiii

Part One: The Quest to Deliver More Value   1
    The "Snowflake" Syndrome   1
    Agile Basics   7
    The Origins of Agile—A Short History   18

Part Two: Diagnosing the Problems   35

    Week 1 – Roles   39
      The Scrum Team   40
      The Product Owner   47
      ScrumMaster   54
      Additional Roles   61
      Stakeholders   62
      Management—A Special Breed of Stakeholder 66
      Combining Scrum Roles   72

    Week 2 – The Product Backlog   79
      Creating Backlog Items   80
      User Story Composition   82
      Determining Priority   89

Organizing the Product Backlog   96
Adding Acceptance Criteria   102
Adding Tasks   107
Determining Doneness   113

Week 3 – Anatomy of a Sprint   **119**
Sprint Planning   120
Daily Scrum   128
Sprint Review   133
Sprint Retrospective   140

Week 4 – Estimation, Commitments, and Project Reporting   **149**
Sprint Commitment—The Scrum Team's Perspective   159
Sprint Commitment—The Product Owner's and
      Stakeholders' Perspectives   168
Managing the Project—The Sprint   176
Managing the Release   184

Week 5 – Creating an Action Plan   **195**
Exploration   196
Coordination   197
Process Definition   199
Strategic Alignment   200
Transformation   201
Plotting a Course for Change   202

Part Three: The Agile Path   **213**

Foreword

As compared to other development methods, agile practices are clear and straightforward. Moreover, it's well documented that organizations adopting these methods are recognizing great value. At CollabNet, we've assisted entire enterprises to reduce development cycles by 75 percent and improve software quality at the team and department level. When extending agile methods to the enterprise, we've seen clients achieve recurring annualized returns in excess of nine figures. But like most changes that yield large value, achieving a successful transition to agile, especially in the enterprise, requires a strong organizational commitment and a number of management and development changes. The time period for this transition can be greatly reduced by getting help in the form of a practical approach from someone that has gone through this journey before you. Most of you realize this—that's why you're reading this book!

When Angela asked me to provide my thoughts regarding the practical approach to agile project management laid out so clearly in this book, I jumped on it. Why? Because she makes two important recurring points:

1. Why reinvent the wheel when getting started? If you can learn from what others have done before, you can avoid some pain. Getting help from an experienced agile coach is key here—someone who can see patterns and behaviors well before a novice can.

2. Enterprise agile transformation is an "in it for the long haul" activity. Developing an ongoing relationship with an agile coach who can provide you with a baseline and consistent feedback on what is going well (or not) is a good idea.

Why do Angela's two principles resonate so well with me? Because her commitment as an Agile Process Mentor to provide leadership, best practices, and stewardship align so well with CollabNet's own vision in which we have sought to provide leadership in the areas of open source, agile methods, and cloud development since the day we founded our company. But even more important, given the increased availability in options for implementing agility from project teams through the enterprise, the need for this external coaching expertise and a set of practical guidelines has never been greater. Please let me elaborate.

When we started CollabNet twelve years ago, we saw that the practices found in agile and open-source-based community processes, tools, and resources could fundamentally transform the way enterprise software was developed. Instead of struggling with disparate and disconnected processes and tools, we recognized that commercial organizations and distributed development teams could realize greater innovation through a set of modern and transparent collaborative practices and processes on a Web-based platform. The results have been impressive. Centralized and collaborative access by global teams to common service resources utilizing "the right set" of development approaches has yielded significant cultural, business, and innovation results.

Today, the need for coordinated enterprise change and company-wide agility is even larger. The convergence of three large-scale industry trends—agile, the integration of development and operations, and the use of external clouds—are combining to create an unprecedented wave of opportunity for the enterprise. These three industry trends are all helping to drive software application lifecycle agility—agility in the selection of agile software development methods used, agility in the way in which development teams and operational teams collaborate throughout the entire software development lifecycle within and among project teams, and the agility to choose and incorporate a mix of internal and external cloud platforms aimed at solving the precise business objectives and technical needs of each specific application under development. This unprecedented organizational flexibility been shown to cut development cycles dramatically, greatly improve quality, and reduce costs as well.

The shift toward these agile methods results in a variety of options that empower developers to choose their specific development processes, platforms, and tools in virtually any geographic location to meet their design objectives. This has led to rapid advances in time to market and quality by project teams, and it enabled them to make rapid and self-empowered decisions around team structure, tooling, processes, and technologies.

The downside to this proliferation of easily available methods available to companies is that, left unmanaged, there can be a proliferation of incompatible tools, processes, and deployment approaches that can grow across the enterprise, causing a surge of development, cost, and visibility issues for management. In today's fast-paced environment with so many available options, development runs the risk of being optimized around project goals and objectives at the expense of organizational-wide improvements leverage. This can result in inconsistent processes and nomenclature, a rash of data format and tool configurations, enterprise architecture integration issues, deployment sprawl, lack of visibility and governance, and employee frustration. In this environment, achieving coordinated development, delivery, and deployment can be difficult. Without close attention to organizational consistency, velocity can decrease, and the application life-cycle costs in a company can actually increase.

So how can an organization integrate these new agile techniques to spur innovation within the project team while simultaneously providing governance and visibility to management? As Angela points out, this balance can be achieved by leveraging the knowhow of coaches that have been there before and a commitment to long-term organizational transformation. In our market, accomplished correctly, CollabNet calls this Enterprise Cloud Development.

Leveraging our experience in distributed open source and agile, CollabNet provides a blueprint for enterprises to achieve the benefits of development and deployment utilizing a mix of on-premise and off-premise teams and IT resources—what industry is now calling a "hybrid cloud" approach to development and deployment. Similar to the principles espoused in this book, this blueprint is a practical five-step approach containing management process and development practices that help companies leverage this hybrid market shift. Essentially, it enables the orchestration of various development and deployment processes across public, private, and on-premise environments.

Regardless of your needs, whether it be the insertion of an agile project management framework like Scrum into your team or across your organization or the adoption of practices that extend agile from development into deployment or the integration of external clouds into your development approach, one thing is certain. Change will be constant. Approaches will continue to evolve in your organization as increasingly diverse teams strive to collaborate and innovate across time zones and geographies. As Angela notes in this book, regardless of to what extent or why an organization moves to agile, the key to success is having the right information at the right time.

Angela's book provides us with the tools to manage this change. She provides us with an approach that is straightforward and which can adapt over time—a list of common problems and some practical approaches and ideas for solving those problems. Based on her years of experience working with scores of organizations, Angela is providing us with a "desk reference" of problems—patterns of issues that arise as an organization gets started with agile and their typical symptoms and the probable root causes. Most important, she helps us by providing a framework that allows us to get started—today.

I encourage you to adopt the practices and the approaches that are laid out in this book. And please know that enterprise agile transformation will take time and commitment. It's a long-haul activity. Augment the principles outlined in this book by developing a long-term relationship with an agile coach who can help you guide your organization, step by step, through the transformation process. He or she will help you recognize the patterns outlined in this book, affect change, and measure your progress in the future. A good agile coach will be a trusted partner for you to enable this transformation and will help you to correctly and rapidly take advantage of the benefits agile can yield.

I want to congratulate Angela on taking the time to document her deep experience in this book. I also want to thank and congratulate not only Angela but also the other Certified Scrum Trainers and practice consultants at CollabNet and across the entire agile community, all of whom continue to push and evolve agile and Scrum practices for the benefit of organizations worldwide. Their work has enabled business, technical, and cultural breakthroughs, helping companies around the world to overcome very real challenges, business obstacles, and market pressures. Their effort has provided the baseline upon which we can continue to work and evolve together as a community as we build new solutions to address the ever-changing IT dynamics.

Bill Portelli
Chief Executive Officer and Chairman
CollabNet

Acknowledgments

To my wonderful husband, Ralph, thank you so much for your patience, support, and keen editorial eye. Your unwavering encouragement is a big part of why this book now exists.

To my friend Dr. Julie Miller, thank you for your excellent class "Business Writing That Counts." Though it has been many years since I took the class, I continue to use the principles you taught us as I create articles, webinars, whitepapers, and now, this book. (You can learn more about Julie's wonderful course here: http://www.businesswritingthatcounts.com)

To Brendon Southam, thank you for your steadfast friendship and for introducing me to the "elegant violence" that is rugby. Also, many thanks for your excellent design and maintenance of the angeladruckman.com website. I am lucky to have such talented friends!

To my colleagues at CollabNet, thank you for the advice, guidance, support, and friendship that you provide. It is a privilege to be part of such a great team.

Finally, and perhaps most of all, I want to extend a very heartfelt thank-you to my clients. Your courage, tenacity, and willingness to work through all the challenges of becoming an agile organization amaze me every day. You make my job the best job in the world.

Part One

The Quest to Deliver More Value

The "Snowflake" Syndrome

You may have tried to implement agile practices like Scrum in your organization. In doing so, you may have experienced some problems. You may think these problems are unique to your company, the products you make, your regulatory situation, or even the people on your teams.

They're not.

In fact, I am going to bet the challenges you are experiencing are very similar to those other organizations face, even those that are very different from your own. When companies adopt agile practices, the problems they experience are remarkable not in their variety but in their similarity. Enterprises in such diverse fields as semiconductors, media, manufacturing, and financial services all struggle with the same questions when adopting an agile framework like Scrum:

- How do I get my teams to self-manage?
- What do I do if my management doesn't support Scrum?
- Who should serve as our Product Owner? How do I get that person to fulfill the role well?
- Why do our sprint-planning meetings take so long?

- When is the right time to include our stakeholders (business people, managers, customers, vendors) in the Scrum process, and what is their role?

The answers to these questions get to the essence of what it means to "do agile"—to integrate agile principles into an organization at its core. And the process of moving from a non-agile state to one where everyone in the organization has fully internalized agile principles is remarkably similar, regardless of the size or type of company involved.

I am an Agile Process Mentor. What does that somewhat vague title mean? Well, part of what it means is that I teach courses that help people to learn about agile product development and how they can use the agile frameworks in their organizations. One such framework is Scrum. Scrum is an agile project management framework that allows teams to deliver smaller bits of valuable, high-quality functionality to the business more rapidly. As a Certified Scrum Trainer (CST), I spend a good deal of time teaching the two-day certification courses that allow people to become recognized as either a Certified ScrumMaster (CSM) or Certified Scrum Product Owner (CSPO).

Instructing for training courses is only part of what I do. Most of the rest of my time is spent working individually with organizations, sometimes only a group or two within a larger enterprise but often on a much more global scale, helping them solve or at least improve upon the specific problems and challenges they are having implementing agile practices. Onsite at their locations, I work with teams, managers, and other stakeholders to improve the results the enterprise is getting from agile.

I have worked with companies of all sizes, from tiny start-ups with fewer than twenty employees to large multi-national corporations. I have also been fortunate to work with enterprises all over the world, from both North and South America to Europe, Asia, and Australia. What I have found is that, while differences do exist, patterns of similarity stand out. When organizations are struggling to adapt to agile practices, their challenges stem from a mostly finite set of root causes. Despite the assurances (which I have heard from my clients many times) of "You don't understand—we have unique challenges!" in fact there is a fairly predictable set of problems that occur when trying to implement an agile framework. I tell them, "Yes, you are unique, just like each snowflake is unique ... but you are still a snowflake, and all snowflakes are much more alike than they are different."

This stems from two basic truths. The first is that, no matter where on the globe you visit, people are people. We all have strengths and weaknesses, likes and dislikes, and varying comfort with change. So the people issues that enterprises tend to have while implementing agile frameworks are fairly universal. They may have slight nuances by geography due to cultural norms but, in general, whether you are in Peoria or Penang, you are likely to find some people who find change energizing and exciting and others who find it stressful and threatening. Such attitudes can have a marked effect on a company's ability to learn new practices effectively.

The other reason that challenges with agile adoption follow a fairly predictable path is that the agile principles themselves are quite simple in structure. They were designed to be frameworks rather than methodologies, lightweight and with a minimum of required artifacts and processes, in order to work for many different kinds of businesses and in many different situations. Because of this inherent simplicity, there are only so many potential root causes for a given symptom. The most prudent course is usually to look for the most obvious issues first, simply because experience shows they are likely to yield the source of the problem. As more experienced doctors tell their interns when making a diagnosis: "When you hear hoof beats, think horses, not zebras."

When I visit an organization to help employees and management with their agile adoption, I might perform one or more of several activities. I may observe the teams themselves in action, noting their communication patterns and ability to self-manage. If the organization is using a framework such as Scrum, I might talk with their ScrumMasters—who facilitate and protect the team—to better understand the problems and issues they face. I may speak with the Product Owners—the individuals who drive product direction and oversee the return on investment of the product—to determine if they understand their role and how to negotiate with the team to be successful in both short- and long-term planning. And I might also talk with the organization's management, helping them understand how to link the activities of each iteration that the team produces with longer-range strategic planning efforts. In every case, I am learning what each group sees as the major issues at hand, looking for common themes, and just as important, noting where differences of opinion exist.

For organizations that are serious about agile transformation and particularly for larger ones, these coaching sessions can be an ongoing process. It is not unusual for me to visit clients regularly, often every few months over a period of years, each time helping them to identify their most pressing problems and how to address them so we can move on to working with other problems in the following visit.

The outcome of these visits, which might be as short as one day but may be much longer for a larger enterprise, is summarized in a document that I call "Observations and Recommendations." But the nickname I like to give it is "The Homework." It contains a synopsis of the patterns I observed during my visit, which ones I think are interfering most directly with the organization's ability to deliver value, and finally, what changes I think the enterprise should work on in the immediate future that will yield the greatest positive result.

What is interesting about these post-visit documents is how much, regardless of the client organization involved, they have in common with one another. True, there are problems unique to certain industries, but in general, impediments in adopting agile practices are amazingly universal. Furthermore, there are themes to the problems companies have in adopting agile practices. Issues do not crop up randomly. Instead, they follow a loosely predictable path that maps to the identifiable stages of agile adoption. Understanding the implementation cycle of agile and where an organization is on that path can be extremely helpful in predicting what problems it is likely to encounter and how best to deal with those issues.

That is the purpose of this book—to make you aware of the common issues and problems at each stage of agile adoption and give you tools and strategies to successfully overcome them.

How to Use This Book

Many years ago, when I was a novice agile practitioner, I bought several of the popular books on the topic to learn more about these new approaches to managing complex projects. But when I actually started to use Scrum and encountered problems, I found the books were less useful to me than I had hoped. They were often written as long narratives or in encyclopedia-style—an exhaustive documentation of every nuance of the framework. It seemed I had to dig through them to find the particular problem I was experiencing, and even when I did locate it, sometimes the advice was either too general or it didn't seem to map well to the particular issues I was experiencing. What I really needed was something more simple and generic—a list of common problems and some practical approaches and ideas for solving those problems.

If you've experienced similar frustrations, this book is for you. It is not meant to be a comprehensive study of all agile methods. Nor is it an exhaustive primer on the finer points of Scrum. Rather, it is something of a desk reference of problems—common issues that arise as an organization gets started with agile, typical symptoms, and the likely root cause. Most important, it will also offer you changes you can begin making today to start improving those problem areas.

Because each reader comes to this book with a different level of experience, it will be useful to read all of Part One. This part of the book has important information about what it means to be agile, its applicability across different kinds of industries and projects, and how to decide when an agile approach is appropriate. For those new to agile concepts and even for experienced practitioners, this can be useful groundwork for the later sections.

Part One also contains a description of the mechanics of Scrum. Though by no means the only approach to doing agile, Scrum has been well-received as a framework for agile project management because of its ability to address common problems experienced when trying to use traditional project management techniques on technology projects. Taking the time to review this section will ensure you understand the language and mechanics of Scrum. It will also make the examples in the book more meaningful.

Time is a valuable commodity. You certainly don't want to read through a whole section, only to discover at the end that the advice doesn't apply to your situation. So Part Two of the book is divided into five sections:

- Roles
- The Product Backlog
- Anatomy of a Sprint
- Estimation, Commitment and Project Reporting

- Creating an Action Plan

The first four sections of Part Two each cover an area in which those new to agile practices typically experience problems. These sections can be read and worked through, one per week if this is an area in which you are struggling. If not, feel free to skip that topic or just skim it. The final section, Week 5, will help you create an action plan for moving forward.

In each section, you will find typical areas where organizations experience problems with agile. Each section begins with a series of questions entitled "Does this sound familiar?" Take a few moments to go through these. If the problems described sound like issues that are occurring in your organization, that chapter will likely hold information you will find useful. If not, you can feel free to skip that chapter or just skim it.

But if you want to do a thorough analysis of your current level of agile adoption, consider taking the time to go through each category and section, carefully considering if any of the problems described are happening in your company. As the title implies, you can cover one section per week, about thirty days in all. But feel free to take it slower as well. Spend more time on the areas that are giving you the most trouble now.

In addition, throughout the book you will also find "Agile Tips." These notes will help you better understand the concepts and terminology used in the agile frameworks. There are many simple words like "done," "impediment," and "acceptance" that mean more in agile than they do in the general language. They will also help you understand some of the more subtle points of agile and how to put them into use.

Ultimately, this book will help you create an action plan. Most organizations have far more problems than they have money or time to fix, and *30 Days to Better Agile* will help you focus your energies where they will do the most good.

This book is designed to give you information you can start using today to improve your agile transformation. Leading change can be hard. Sometimes it may feel as if you are the only person who sees the problems that currently exist in your organization. Or maybe you feel as if you are the only one who is willing to do something about it. But, rest assured, others have traveled this path before. There is nothing new under the sun. You can make your life a lot easier by learning from others' victories and missteps. If my experiences coaching agile teams can help improve your experiences as you continue along your agile journey, then both your time and mine will have been well spent.

Agile Basics

What Does It Mean to Be "Agile"?

- *"We can't do agile because we are in a heavily regulated industry and have to do lots of documentation."*

- *"Agile uses self-managed teams—so that means they do whatever they feel like."*

- *"We don't do planning. We're agile!"*

> **Agile Tip**
>
> Though agile methods can be used for any type of complex work, they are ideally suited to new-product development.

There are many misconceptions about what the term "agile" means when applied to software development and, on a greater scale, to new product development. So let's take a moment and agree on a definition:

Agile Product Development—a conceptual framework for developing new products that seeks to minimize risk and maximize value delivered by working in time-boxed iterations and emphasizing working product as a primary measure of success.

A few of the phrases in the definition above need a little more clarification. First, note that the agile approaches are referred to as "frameworks" rather than "structured methodologies." This is because they are designed to be lightweight and work well in a variety of types of organizations. The required processes, meetings, and artifacts of agile methods are kept to a minimum, understanding that each enterprise will have different requirements in this area. This means the agile frameworks, unlike more structured and artifact-heavy approaches, can work equally well for small start-ups and large multi-national organizations.

> **Agile Tip**
>
> A timebox is a pre-defined amount of time in which to achieve a given result. With agile, the emphasis is not in adding more time (to a meeting or project) but using the time available well.

Agile methods are also particularly well suited to the development of new-products. In new product development, the end state is often unknown at the outset of the project. These efforts are often an exploration of what is possible. The iterative approach of agile product development allows for a discovery process throughout the project. While there is nothing wrong with using an agile approach for system maintenance, for example, it is a particularly powerful approach to use when venturing into the unknown territory of new-product development.

Outside of the development of new products, an agile approach is also useful when a project, for whatever reason, has a great deal of uncertainty. Technological complications, changing client requirements, and rapidly changing business climates are all examples of uncertainty. An agile approach, with its frequent inspect-and-adapt cycles, provides a clear and timely way to fold in new requirements as they make themselves known. It is no surprise that the agile methods were popularized in the area of software development, where nearly every project has a considerable amount of uncertainty in either requirements or technology.

Agile methods also value the use of a timebox to define an iteration of work. In a way, this is exactly the opposite approach taken with traditional methods of project management. Traditional project management states: "Here is the work I want done. How long will it take to complete it?" An agile approach instead asks: "This is how much time I have—how much high-value functionality can I get in that time?" It is a subtle but important difference. Time-boxing is an important skill because, in business and life in general, time is often our most limited resource. Being able to deliver the maximum value possible in the given amount of time can translate into a serious competitive advantage.

 Now that we have a working definition for what agile product development is, it is worth noting what it is not. Being agile does *not* mean changing direction every five minutes. Nor does it mean proceeding blindly forward without a plan. Agile teams do have the ability to respond to changes in business requirements in order to provide more value, but they do so in a structured way. The single word I would associate with good agile teams is discipline. Agile organizations use a disciplined approach combined with the responsiveness of empirical techniques to make the best decisions possible with the information known at the time.

Empirical Versus Predictive Project Management

There are many project-management frameworks and methodologies in use in the business world. Most of them will produce good results at least some of the time. Unfortunately, most of them can (and do) fail spectacularly when used in conditions for which they are not well suited. So how do we know what approach to use on a given project? And how do these considerations play into an organization's desire to adopt agile practices?

The answer lies in having a clear and accurate assessment of the type of project under consideration. By matching a project to a management approach that addresses its key challenges and risks, organizations can vastly improve their odds of success. Most important, choosing the correct approach for the project you are starting helps you avoid the trap of generating data and statistics about project progress that are misleading.

Consider the traditional gated project-management approach. Sometimes called the "waterfall" approach, this project-management style is predictive in nature, meaning it tries to reduce risk by making accurate predictions about future events in the project. Such methods usually follow a phased approach to product development, whether the organization is building software, automobiles, or kitchen appliances. Typical phases are:

- Requirements gathering
- Design
- Development or construction
- Testing and quality assurance
- Deployment or release

> **Agile Tip**
>
> Traditional project-management methods such as waterfall are only effective at risk control when the requirements will not change over the life of the project.

You can probably see where the waterfall approach gets its name: the output of each phase flows into the next phase. The phases also operate quite independently. If I am a designer, for example, my customer is the development group. The output of my work flows to its members, and I would very rarely have anything to do with, for example, the testing group, as it is further downstream from the stage at which I am involved with the project.

This process of handing off work between groups that function essentially independently from each other has been likened to the way a group of runners might compete as a relay team. In a relay race, each person performs his or her work independently. The key point of interaction between team members is when the baton is passed from one runner to another. Similarly, in waterfall development, the formal communication points between team members tend to be centered on the hand-off points. In other words, if I am a software developer on a waterfall project, I have little interest in or involvement with requirements gathering. Nor would I have much interest in or ability to contribute to the project until the work progresses further downstream.

Not surprisingly, there can be serious weaknesses to this project-management approach. The first issue is its strong reliance on gathering and articulating the requirements up front. Devoting the time and money to have a full effort in requirements gathering at the start of a project is only effective if the organization has good reason to believe that those parameters will not change. But if, as is so often true with new-product development or projects that have a great deal of uncertainty, the list of requirements is not fixed, and this approach immediately incurs more cost and risk. The requirements document is passed on to designers and developers who begin making technical decisions based on a set of assumptions associated with the defined requirements. When those requirements change, organizations can find themselves with an inflexible solution that no longer meets the newly discovered needs.

Lack of ability to incorporate emerging requirements is only part of the problem with a waterfall approach. Even assuming minimal changes in requirements, there are still problems that stem from the nature of how workgroups are formed and how information is passed from one group to another. As in our relay-race example above, workgroups in a waterfall-style enterprise tend to be divided across job titles. All the software developers might be in one group, the business analysts in another, and the user-interface designers in still another. In such an organization, problems invariably stem from the handoff points between groups. Because there is no team that takes responsibility for delivering an entire unit of functionality, when communication breaks down (as it often does because of the lack of interaction between groups) and problems occur, there is no one who possesses a global view that can allow him or her to take responsibility for choosing the best path to resolution. Individuals who work in the quality assurance (or QA) area of an organization are very familiar with this pattern. They know that whoever is left holding the bag last is blamed when the project is late. Hence, the complaint from some software developers, "QA made our project late again!"

If these situations where unknown requirements can derail a project are not well suited to a waterfall approach, is there another technique for managing such projects? In fact, this is the ideal situation for an empirical approach such as the agile method. Rather than relying on up-front predictions, an agile approach acknowledges that many unknowns exist at the beginning of the project. Therefore, the agile frameworks use an empirical approach of inspect-and-adapt cycles to discover and capture new information as it makes itself known. The graphic below illustrates some of the key differences between the two approaches:

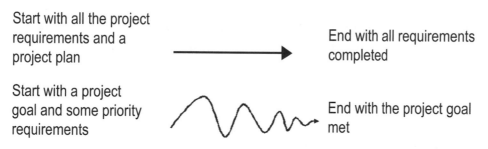

Start with all the project requirements and a project plan → End with all requirements completed

Start with a project goal and some priority requirements → End with the project goal met

As is implied from the graphic, the starting points of the two approaches are quite different. With a predictive method such as the waterfall style (the top graphic), having an exhaustive documentation of all the requirements is key. Indeed, this phase of the project often culminates in the creation of a requirements document, which must be signed by the customer in order for work to proceed. After agreeing upon all the requirements, a good project manager then uses that information to create a project plan, which contains detailed information about staffing needs, work breakdown (tasks), and critical path. As an example, if this were a software-development project, actual software development would begin after the creation and approval of the requirements document. And the goal of such a project is to end with all the requirements completed. Indeed, it can often be a formalized step in project approval to sit down with the customer and review, line by line, the requirements document, showing how and where in the product each requirement has been fulfilled.

An agile approach, by contrast, is quite different in both its starting point and ultimate destination. Rather than an extensive list of requirements, an agile approach can and must begin with a project goal. A project goal is a high-level description of the desired end-state of the project, with very little information about how to get there. But a project goal is not quite enough to get started. An agile project needs a few requirements, often key ones, which are primary in the customer's mind. These initial requirements put a "stake in the ground" and give teams a starting point. At this point, using our software development example above, teams are ready to begin building product. Understandably, the early efforts in such an approach yield new requirements, which can often change the direction of the project, sometimes quite radically. Therefore, progress can feel somewhat more disjointed with an agile approach, particularly early in the project. A team may create a product in which the business, upon seeing the working modules, discovers new features and functionality it wants. But unlike a predictive approach, whose value as a risk-control model lessens with every new change, an agile approach welcomes such changes. With agile, we have not "bet the farm" too early and made design decisions that will trap us later on. Rather, we let the best plan emerge, always keeping a firm handle on reaching the project goal but staying flexible in how we do that.

A real-life example will be helpful. Imagine you are in charge of planning your family's two-week summer vacation this year. You might have a project goal something like this: "Plan and deliver a two-week summer vacation that four family members, ages seven to thirty-nine will enjoy and find memorable." You need to decide how best to approach this project. One way would be to take a predictive approach. You might interview each family member, gathering his or her requirements, a list of which might look something like this:

- Go to an amusement park
- Visit Aunt Marge
- Stay in nice hotels
- Stay within the United States

- Spend at least two days at the beach doing fun activities

If you feel confident that these requirements are both well understood and will not change, a predictive approach could work quite well for this project. There seems to be a theme to the trip—it sounds like a typical vacation any number of families might take in a given summer. It should be quite a simple effort to plan a two-week trip with time at an amusement park and the beach and still have a bit of time left over to visit with Aunt Marge.

But even this simple list of requirements is fraught with potential problems and misunderstandings. What if your family members (who we would call "stakeholders" in the business environment) have different ideas about which amusement park they want to visit? What if Aunt Marge is going to be vacationing herself at the time of your visit and won't be home? And what are "fun" activities to do at the beach? What if one family member's idea of fun is lying in the sun reading a book and another thinks of going paragliding as fun? Even more challenging, what if a new opportunity arises—how do you take advantage of it? For example, what if Aunt Marge decides to spend the summer in France and invites you to join her, all expenses paid? If you stick rigorously to your list of requirements above, you will find that new information, as it makes itself known, makes it increasingly difficult and often undesirable to remain bound by the requirements that you identified early in the project.

Agile methods are ideal for such projects where maintaining a flexible approach is of high value. In our example, your project goal—"plan and deliver a two-week summer vacation that four family members, ages seven to thirty-nine will enjoy and find memorable"—would remain the same, but rather than trying to define an exhaustive list of requirements, you would focus on key requirements that were known and let the rest emerge as you got further into the planning process. The agile approach would allow new opportunities, such as the prospect of spending time in France, to be integrated into the total solution, making the overall output of the project of more value.

Agile Tip

Agile methods recognize the concept of *emerging requirements*—those requirements that are not and often cannot be known at the beginning of a project.

In business, perhaps the most important difference between predictive and empirical approaches is their desired end states. With a predictive approach, the goal is to end with all the requirements met. With an empirical approach, the desire is to finish the project with the project goal met, regardless of which requirements were or were not met. This may seem like a subtle difference, but in practice it can be a dramatic one. With a predictive approach, particularly for projects that last a long time, business continues to change even as the requirements on the list remain static. Unhappy teams taking this approach may have the misfortune to hear, "Yes, that's what I asked for, but it is not what I need anymore…" Such projects are in a Catch-22: the business's needs have continued to evolve and change. If the requirements don't change with them, teams run the risk of building "shelfware"—a product that no one will use because the features it contains are no longer useful. Yet every new requirement that is folded in weakens the original predictions about project scope, duration, etc., and as we said earlier, the ability to make accurate predictions is the main strength of this approach.

With all that being said, is a waterfall approach bad? In fact, the answer is no. Predictive approaches like waterfall work quite well when you have good reason to believe you can make accurate predictions. This means they work well for projects that are low risk, short, and non-exploratory in nature. But when risk starts to rear its ugly head in the form of uncertainty, an agile approach is a better choice.

The graphic on the next page helps illustrate this. Note the diagram has two variables or factors it uses to predict the type of project you are facing. The x-axis is noted as "technology," and you will see it spans from "low risk" in the lower left of the graph to "high risk" on the far right. This range represents a measure of project risk from a technological perspective. What causes a project to incur technological risk? Anything that creates uncertainty from a technological perspective. For example, let's say you are enhancing an existing software product for a small, finite number of users. You have many developers who understand this system and have worked on it before. You might define this project as having a low technological risk.

On the other hand, perhaps you are building a large, new product. The total number of end users is hard to estimate. There are several, as-yet-undefined connection points with third-party software and client systems. Even worse, the technology being used to build the system is new to your team. A project such as this might be described as having high technological risk.

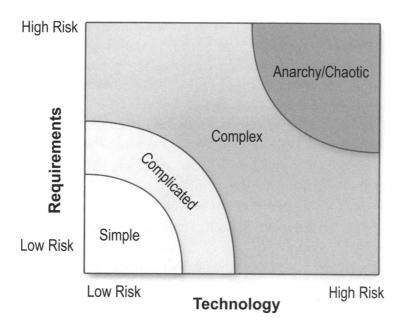

Evaluating System Complexity

The y-axis, noted as "requirements" can be interpreted in a similar way. Projects whose requirements are well understood and not changing are said to have a lower requirements risks. But when there is uncertainty in requirements, the risk elevates.

Even in the next section of the graph, which is described as "complicated," a predictive approach can still yield good results. True, some uncertainty does exist. But a complicated project is defined as one in which, at the beginning of the project, more is known than unknown. So a predictive approach with some mechanisms for folding in the new changes that do occur is often an effective approach.

What about the far upper right of the graph, the area denoted as "anarchy/chaotic"? Does an agile approach help you there? Usually, the answer is no. These are projects where there is extremely high uncertainty in both technology and requirements. In other words, you don't know what you are aiming for (requirements risk). Nor do you know how you will get there (technology risk). The reason agile won't help you here is that projects in this state often lack a project goal. Either they are wandering research efforts, or they feel a bit more like a blind panic. If you've ever worked on a project where the customer didn't know what he or she wanted, only that it (whatever "it" ended up being when requirements were finally known) had to be delivered by March 1 or else, you understand the nature of a chaotic project.

Unsurprisingly, a predictive approach won't help much, either, in such situations. Ironically, this is one type of project that can actually benefit from a leader taking a bit of a command-and-control approach. Think of a group of five-year olds in their very first season of soccer practice. A coach in such a situation will likely take a fairly structured approach to helping these children learn the game. When the athletes become more experienced, though, he may allow them more freedom to structure some elements of their practices themselves. Having a central point of command can help introduce order into such a project, reducing chaos and effectively moving the project down and to the left of the graph.

So if an agile approach can't magically fix any of the problems we've described above, when is it the right choice? An empirical approach like agile is an ideal choice for the large gray area of the graph described as "complex." Complex projects are ones in which, at the beginning, more is unknown than known. There is a moderate- to high-level of uncertainty in the project. Not the black-hole uncertainty of the chaotic project but far more risk than the areas to the lower left of the graph. An agile approach, with its built-in cycles of inspect and adapt, is a perfect choice for managing the risk of complex projects.

This information can be particularly important when considering the first agile projects an organization attempts. The best opportunities for making full use of the power of agile while reaping the highest benefits of risk control are on complex projects. While it might be tempting to make your first foray into agile with a very-low-risk project (and you can do that if the effort is strictly meant as a learning exercise), you will likely find that the benefits of an agile approach over one that is more predictive are limited. Likewise, an agile approach is unlikely to save a project in anarchy.

Agile Tip

A project goal describes the end state a project is trying to achieve. It can be likened to a target at which all activities of the project are aimed. The requirements, which are like the path to that target, can vary. But when the target itself begins to move, the project is in jeopardy

Until an agile team has a target at which to aim in the form of a project goal, they cannot effectively use the framework to add value.

Is an Agile Approach a Good Choice for Your Project?

Use the following guidelines to decide if your project would benefit from an agile project management approach:

1. Can you define a project goal?

   - If yes, agile may be right for this project
   - If no, agile may not be the best approach

2. Is your technological risk:

   - High—agile may be right for this project
   - Medium—agile may be right for this project
   - Low—agile may be overkill

3. Is your requirement risk:

   - High—agile may be right for this project
   - Medium—agile may be right for this project
   - Low—agile may be overkill for this project

4. Do you feel that there is a significant number of unknowns in this project?

   - If yes, agile may be right for this project

5. Is this a troubled project (i.e., one that has been attempted unsuccessfully before)?

   - If yes, agile may be right for this project

For these reasons, because the agile frameworks are inherently designed to work for higher risk projects, it is not unusual for the approach to be used as a last-resort on problem projects. Indeed, even for their very first foray into agile, many organizations decide to use an agile approach on a project only after they've tried a number of other approaches without success. In fact, troubled projects can be great candidates for agile projects. Team members are weary and often have the attitude, "We may as well try this new agile thing because what we're doing now sure isn't working very well!" Having this "nothing to lose and everything to gain" attitude can help team members be open to learning the skills required to be successful with agile.

The Origins of Agile—A Short History

As we saw earlier, it comes as no surprise that the agile frameworks gained popularity in the software industry. The inherent risk involved in building technologically complex projects made this industry ripe for an approach that could effectively manage a great deal of change. But the origins of agile— where the concepts really formed and took hold—are actually in the area of manufacturing material goods like automobiles, cameras, and copiers.

In 1986, professors Hirotaka Takeuchi and Ikujiro Nonaka published an article in the *Harvard Business Review* entitled, "The New, New Product Development Game." In this article, the professors observed that the skills required to successfully create new, innovative products required a special way of organizing work. Unlike the structured, gated approach to coordinating work between individual contributors that was popular at the time, teams that excelled in new product development had some unique characteristics. They were comfortable working with ambiguous goals and a high level of uncertainly. They tended to "swarm" on problems, working together as a unit, rather than each individual doing his or her part and then handing it off to the next in line.

Managers in these organizations were different too. Rather than interacting with staff solely by giving orders and directives, they used more subtle methods to allow teams to come to their own conclusions. They redefined failure, understanding that forays into uncharted areas of business naturally meant that not all ideas or attempts would be successful. Such empowerment gave the teams a sense of ownership over both the project and the

Where does the term "Scrum" come from?

The use of the term "Scrum" to describe an approach to agile software development has its origins in "The New, New Product Development Game." In that article, the authors pointed out the ineffectiveness of using a rigid, structured "relay race" approach to new product development. Instead, they argued, teams that excelled at new-product development maintained a much more flexible approach, with an emphasis less on individuals and more on the progress of the work itself. In such flexibility, they found another apt sports analogy: rugby.

Though it is still an emerging sport in the United States, rugby is wildly popular in many parts of the world, especially northern Europe, South Africa, Australia, and New Zealand. While at first glance, rugby may look a bit like American football, there is one rule that makes it a completely different game: rugby does not allow forward passing. Therefore, a team, made up of fifteen players, must work together to pass the ball laterally or backwards many, many times in an effort to work their way down the field and score.

Professors Takeuchi and Nonaka saw in rugby an ideal metaphor for the kind of teamwork they observed in teams that excelled at new product development. The ball represented the work of the project itself, and like a rugby team, agile teams worked together to achieve forward progress, regardless of the achievements of any one particular team member.

In rugby, a "scrum" is a way to restart the ball into play. The agile software development framework Scrum adopted this name due to a similar approach to restarting the work of the project in its sprint-planning meeting.

product itself. They became personally invested in doing the right thing. This organizational approach created highly motivated teams that produced outstanding results.

Though this early research was in the area of manufacturing, it did not go unnoticed by the software industry. Indeed, as early as 1957, software professionals had begun experimenting with iterative software design. This interest in a new, more effective way to create software peaked in 2001, when a group of like-minded software professionals came together to create the

Agile Manifesto. This document aimed to describe a set of principles and values that corresponded with agile software development. These values place a higher emphasis on:

- Individuals and interactions over processes and tools
- Working software over comprehensive documentation
- Customer collaboration over contract negotiation
- Responding to change over following a plan

Practitioners were experimenting with these concepts: working in an iterative fashion, optimizing their work for flexibility, and focusing on high-quality, usable end products.

Such experimentation gave birth to what would become the popular agile frameworks we know today. These early pioneers rejected the heavyweight methods that were currently popular because they felt those techniques had been proven not to work well with software development projects. Instead, they experimented with more lightweight methods that emphasized the values described in "The New, New Product Development Game," namely, self-organizing teams, an iterative, overlapping approach to product development, and a commitment to sharing information throughout the organization. Because of its ability to support these goals within a project-management framework, one such framework that quickly gained popularity is Scrum.

Scrum and Agile

Scrum is an agile project-management framework. In essence, it is part of the agile family, as are eXtreme Programming, Crystal, and Feature-Driven Development. While it is by no means the only agile framework in use today, it is by far the most popular. While organizations may use other approaches to ensure technical quality or for modeling techniques, they consistently turn to Scrum for agile project management. There are several reasons for Scrum's popularity. Scrum is:

- **Easy to understand**—the rules and structure of Scrum are relatively simple to learn. This means organizations can quickly get started with it and begin using the techniques to gain immediate benefits.

- **Lightweight**—like most of the agile frameworks, Scrum is a "low ceremony" approach to project management. There is not a lot of documentation, gates, or other rule structures in the approach. This means Scrum can work equally well for large and small organizations and in a variety of industries.

- **Focused on results**—Scrum emphasizes the delivery of working software (or whatever product you are delivering) as opposed to the creation of project artifacts, such as documentation. Contrary to popular belief, Scrum is not "anti-documentation." It merely proposes that artifacts like documentation should be created only when they serve the greater goal of delivering a usable product.

Because of Scrum's widespread popularity, the examples in this book will, in large part, refer to projects that used Scrum. But the ideas and patterns discussed can really be applied to any kind of iterative product development.

Scrum Basics

Along with many other activities in life—losing weight, saving money—doing Scrum is very simple in theory but somewhat more complex to put into action, let alone to master. While this book is not meant to be an extensive study of the Scrum framework, it is important we establish a common understanding of the basics of Scrum, particularly the roles, inspect-and-adapt points, and the artifacts.

Scrum Roles

There are three Scrum roles. Within each role, it is useful to understand both what that role is designed to produce and what key activities people in those roles perform. It is important to understand the difference between these two points. Scrum roles are designed with checks and balances in mind. While the individuals in each of the Scrum roles are working toward a common goal of creating a high-quality, high-value result, in reality the final product is a product of clearly delineated responsibilities. While many of the Scrum activities—writing user stories, creating acceptance criteria, attending daily Scrums—benefit from active participation of each of the roles, there is, nevertheless, a clear sense of who owns what. This strong sense of ownership is one reason using the Scrum framework can produce such high quality results. The Scrum roles use both shared goals and a healthy sense of keeping each other honest to arrive at what is ultimately a better end result than any one person could have achieved on his or her own.

The Product Owner

The Product Owner is responsible for understanding and articulating the overall vision of the product. He is also responsible for monitoring the costs incurred by the project and the benefits received and making certain the benefits outweigh the costs. In essence, the Product Owner owns the "what," meaning what features and functions end up being in the finished product.

To fulfill these duties, the Product Owner works with groups both inside and outside the Scrum team. To understand the requirements for the product, he will work with stakeholders to gather and articulate these requirements. Stakeholders are any individuals or groups who have a vested interest in the product being created. Stakeholders may be end customers; they may also be management, downstream groups, vendors, or any other of a number of parties. A good Product Owner listens carefully to the needs of all stakeholders and weighs their desires against the need to monitor costs and benefits. Product Owners often have to make tough choices, and that can include sometimes telling stakeholders "no" or at least "not yet."

Product Owners also work directly with the Scrum team to clarify requirements and make commitments for a given iteration, or sprint. At the end of each sprint, the Product Owner has the opportunity to examine the work the team has completed to determine if it meets the agreed-upon level of doneness. Finally, it is the Product Owner who decides if a project should continue for another sprint.

Agile Tip

In Scrum, the Product Owner has ultimate responsibility for doing the "right thing," meaning making certain the product has the necessary features and functionality. The team is responsible for doing the "thing right," meaning ensuring technical quality.

The Scrum Team

Scrum teams are in the business of making and meeting commitments. Recent Scrum literature has softened the word "commitment" to "forecast." This change was, no doubt, an effort to emphasize that a commitment from the team at the beginning of a sprint is only as good as the information on which it is based. If the team is missing key information or if the Product Owner changes his mind, these factors can significantly affect a sprint's outcome.

At the beginning of each sprint, the team looks at the Product Owner's product backlog, a list of prioritized requirements to determine how many of those requirements they can commit to deliver in the upcoming sprint. The team may negotiate with the Product Owner about the scope of the individual requirements themselves, defining acceptance criteria that will help them and their Product Owner know when the requirement is completed. They may also estimate the individual requirements in an effort to better evaluate how many they can take on in a given sprint. Ultimately, it is the team and the team alone that will decide how much the members can commit to in a given sprint.

Once Scrum teams make a commitment to deliver a specific set of requirements in a given sprint, they are free to go about that work however they feel best. Scrum teams often swarm on a set of requirements, meaning they work together as a group to decide both how to approach solving the problem technically as well as how best to divide the work. Whereas the Product Owner owns the "what," meaning he or she has ultimate control over what features are and are not included in a given product, Scrum teams own the "how" and the "how much." As professionals with specialized knowledge, they are in the best position, once a commitment has been made, to determine how best to fulfill it. They do not need a manager or other authority figure to assign work to them. Once a Sprint commitment is made, the team is left to its own devices to decide how to meet that commitment. Because of this, it is said that Scrum teams are self-organizing. If they encounter problems or impediments that they are unable to solve themselves, their ScrumMaster helps remove those problems so the team can remain focused on delivering their commitment.

The ScrumMaster

The ScrumMaster's role has two general components: an inward-facing role and an outward-facing role. The inward-facing part of a ScrumMaster's role is all about facilitation and coaching. A ScrumMaster will support and facilitate the team. She will often act as a facilitator in Scrum meetings, encouraging the good use of time and helping make sure everyone gets a chance to participate fully. The ScrumMaster will also work in partnership with the Product Owner to remove impediments and to support the team in its quest to meet its commitment. Sometimes there are conflicts between a Scrum team and Product Owner, and the ScrumMaster can help with that as well, facilitating productive discussion and working towards a mutually agreeable solution. The Product Owner owns the "what" of a project, and the team owns the "how," but the ScrumMaster owns the process itself.

The outward facing component of the ScrumMaster's role involves working with the outside organization, meaning those stakeholders and other parties outside the Scrum inner circle. A ScrumMaster may take responsibility for doing the project reporting and working with management to understand

Is a ScrumMaster a project manager?

While at first glance the roles may seem similar, the ScrumMaster's and project manager's roles are very different. Project managers are tasked with ensuring the ultimate overall success of a project. It is often embedded into their annual goals and objectives to deliver projects "on time and within budget."

In contrast, a ScrumMaster's ultimate responsibility is to shepherd the process. She does not have responsibility to ensure the project is delivering the right requirements—that belongs to the Product Owner. Nor does she have responsibility to make commitments to deliver work—that belongs to the team. A ScrumMaster's role is deliberately lacking in authority to ensure there is a neutral party overseeing the process itself. Project managers can make the transition to a ScrumMaster's role, but not without changing both some key behaviors as well as what the organization is expecting from them.

what data they need from the project to make good business decisions. She will also work with outside groups affected by the project to help them understand how Scrum works and how their own workgroups may be affected. Ultimately, a ScrumMaster drives organizational change. She helps the organization plot a course from where it is today—which may be decidedly non-agile—to where it wants to be when it has fully embraced the agile values and behaviors.

> **Agile Tip**
>
> The Scrum inner circle is comprised of the ScrumMaster, Product Owner, and Scrum team.

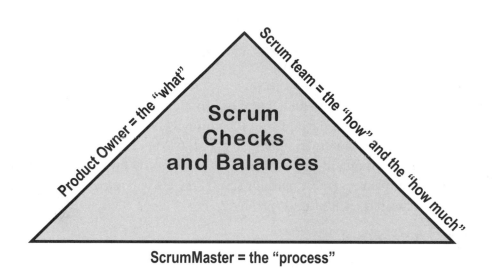

Pigs and Chickens?

In early Scrum literature, roles are sometimes described in terms of whether they are "pig" or "chicken" roles. These playful nicknames were attempting to show that, in Scrum, there are roles that have inherent responsibility in the Scrum process and there are roles that are merely interested in outcomes. The analogy comes from the following old joke:

Pig and Chicken were going to open a restaurant together. "I know," says Chicken. "Let's call our establishment 'Bacon and Eggs,' and then that's what we will serve." Pig looked doubtfully at his friend. "I don't think so," he said. "You would only be involved, but I would actually be committed!"

Most people find these terms outdated and a little silly, but the concepts remain. The ScrumMaster, Product Owner, and Scrum team have commitments in the Scrum process. All other stakeholders, while interested in the project outcome, remain outside this inner circle.

Scrum Inspect-and-Adapt Points

As an empirical approach to project management, Scrum relies on frequent inspect-and-adapt points to fold in new information as it makes itself known. These meetings are an opportunity for the Product Owner, ScrumMaster, and Scrum team—and sometimes other stakeholders—to come together for the purpose of planning and sharing ideas. There are only four official Scrum meetings—the planning meeting, daily scrum, review, and retrospective—and each has a specific result it must produce.

Sprint Planning

The purpose of the sprint planning meeting—that is, what it must produce—is a sprint commitment (or, if you prefer, forecast). The Product Owner comes to this meeting with a list of prioritized requirements—the product backlog—and it is the team's job to determine how many of those requirements they can commit to deliver in the upcoming sprint. To accomplish this end, the Scrum team will attempt to clarify requirements, adding acceptance criteria—boundaries around the scope of the individual requirements—to each one until they feel confident they understand the scope of the requirement.

Once acceptance criteria are established, the team may also estimate the effort involved in fulfilling each requirement to better judge whether or not to make a commitment to specific ones. They may also take the time to lay out the tasks associated with fulfilling each requirement. All of these activities contribute to a team's goal of making a sprint commitment to the Product Owner. Once a commitment has been made, the team then works together to determine how to meet it. When the sprint planning concludes, the team has made a commitment to the Product Owner to deliver a number of his highest priority requirements, and they also have at least begun planning how they will deliver on that commitment. Sprint-planning meetings typically happen on the first day of a sprint. Like all Scrum meetings, sprint-planning meetings are time-boxed. Longer sprints (for example, four weeks) require longer planning meetings than short sprints (such as one week). In general, it is not unusual for teams to become more effective in planning meetings over time and, therefore, have shorter meetings.

Daily Scrum

With an empirical method such as Scrum, there is a need to have a daily checkpoint for the team to coordinate their work efforts and evaluate their progress towards meeting the sprint commitment. This is the purpose of the daily Scrum. Unlike a traditional project-status meeting, where team members report their individual progress to an authority figure such as a project manager, a daily Scrum is for team members to report to each other so they can understand potential impacts and touchpoints between each member's work. Daily Scrum meetings are limited to fifteen minutes, so some efficiency is required. Typically, each team member presents her update in terms of:

- What she has accomplished since the last daily Scrum
- What she is working on today
- Any impediments or issues she is experiencing

The ScrumMaster is there to hear impediments and follow up on them after the daily Scrum. If the team is struggling to keep their

Agile Tip

The Scrum meetings are an important part of the empirical process. Each one is an opportunity to inspect the process and make adaptations. Scrum meetings are always time-boxed.

update succinct, the ScrumMaster can help keep the conversation focused through more active facilitation. Many teams find their daily Scrums are kept to fifteen minutes if they conduct the meeting standing up, rather than sitting around a conference table. For this reason, daily Scrums are sometimes called "daily stand-ups" or "stand-up meetings."

Sprint Review

A sprint review is held at the end of each sprint. The purpose of this meeting is to gain agreement on doneness between the team and Product Owner. The Scrum team will present each requirement they have completed to the Product Owner. They will read the acceptance criteria that were agreed upon with the Product Owner to call that requirement done. In essence, they are giving the Product Owner evidence that he should accept the requirement as complete. If the Product Owner agrees, the requirement is considered done and is potentially shippable, meaning it is ready to be delivered to customers if the Product Owner wants to release it. If the Product Owner does not agree that the requirement has been completed, he will reject the requirement. It will then go back into the product backlog, where it can be re-prioritized according to the Product Owner's wishes.

The sprint-review meeting is somewhat unusual in that it is one of the only Scrum meetings where stakeholders are welcome. If the Product Owner desires, stakeholders may attend the sprint review to see the progress being made on the product and offer ideas and suggestions for future requirements to add to the product backlog. Giving stakeholders the opportunity to see incremental progress on the project—to see parts of it actually working and to give feedback—is often mentioned as one of the key benefits stakeholders, particularly non-technical ones, say they like about the Scrum framework.

Sprint Retrospective

The final Scrum meeting is the sprint retrospective. The purpose of this meeting is to improve the team's working processes. This is primarily a meeting for the Scrum team to talk about how the last sprint went, to discuss how the project or release is going in general, and to identify any changes or improvements they would like to implement in the next sprint. Unlike a lessons-learned meeting at the end of a traditionally managed project, the results of the retrospective are quite targeted. The team may identify many issues, approaches, or impediments they hope to change at some point. But from that list, they will typically pick one or two things to try in the next sprint. By limiting changes, they can evaluate the results of the proposed change to decide if they want to continue in that direction or take another approach.

The planning, daily scrum, review, and retrospective are the only required Scrum meetings. But in practice, Product Owners and Scrum teams often find they also need regular working sessions together to refine and better understand the product backlog. These meetings, often called Story-Time or, more generically, product backlog grooming sessions, help with this. Often held every sprint, a few days before planning, these meetings give the Product Owner, ScrumMaster, and Scrum team an opportunity to improve the backlog by breaking down large requirements, adding detail, and even estimating. Holding regular product backlog grooming sessions both improves the effectiveness of the subsequent planning meeting and tends to make it take less time.

Is Scrum a methodology?

In the most generic sense, because Scrum is a set of principles and practices, it could be referred to as a methodology. But in the practical sense, Scrum lacks the structured approach of more predictive methods. It is often referred to as a "management wrapper" that can be placed around other activities and processes the organization finds useful. Scrum does not intend to provide all the answers for every problem that may occur in a project. For this reason, we will refer to Scrum as a method or framework, rather than a methodology.

Scrum Artifacts

As with all agile frameworks, Scrum keeps required documentation to a minimum. Depending on an individual organization's needs, it may need or choose to supplement these artifacts with additional documentation, reports, and other useful information. But the product backlog, sprint backlog, and burndown charts are the ones found in nearly all Scrum projects.

Product Backlog

The product backlog is a list in priority order of all physical and intellectual property and services requested by the Product Owner. It is important to note that a list of requirements cannot be considered a product backlog until it is prioritized. This is key because the Scrum team will make commitments to the Product Owner working from the top of the product backlog downward. If the team, for example, can commit only to items 1–4 on a product backlog, they can do so confident that they are delivering the four items that will bring the highest value to the business.

It is the Product Owner's responsibility to prioritize the product backlog. He will evaluate each backlog item and position it so as to bring the greatest benefit at that point in time. The product backlog is a living document. A Product Owner can and should revise the backlog each sprint, making any necessary adjustments, additions, or removals. It is important to note that, unlike a traditional requirements document, a product backlog does not represent all the work the project will deliver. Instead, at any given moment, it represents all the work the Product Owner hopes to get. After every sprint, the Product Owner makes a judgment as to whether doing an additional sprint will yield enough value to justify the cost. If the answer is yes, another sprint ensues. But it is not unusual for a Product Owner to decide, even though items still remain in the backlog, to end a project. In such cases, the remaining items were either determined to be "nice to haves" rather than "must haves" or they will be included in some future release.

Sprint Backlog/Sprint Commitment

As we said earlier, the purpose of the sprint-planning meeting is for the team to make a sprint commitment. Once they commit to delivering a given number of product backlog items, teams often find it useful to determine the tasks they will need to perform to deliver this work. A sprint backlog contains the committed requirements for an individual sprint, along with the tasks needed to fulfill those requirements. Whereas the requirement in the product backlog is a description of *what* needs to be delivered, the tasks describe *how* that requirement will be fulfilled.

Teams may keep their sprint backlog in an electronic tool designed especially to support Scrum projects. They may also use a physical task board.

Typically occupying a wall of the team room, a physical task board is often made of simple tools—index cards or Post-it notes—that show each requirement the team has committed to deliver and its associated tasks. The tasks then exist in one of three states: not started, meaning no one on the team is actively working on that task yet; in process, meaning the task is actively being worked; and done, meaning the task has been completed.

When teams use physical task boards, they often have their daily Scrum at the board, moving items into the "done" column as they are completed and into the "in process" column as team members start work on tasks. If teams use an electronic tool to track their progress, updates must happen in a similar manner.

Burndown Charts

Throughout the sprint, the Scrum team, Product Owner, and ScrumMaster are constantly monitoring the health of the sprint and if they are on track to meet the sprint commitment. One tool they use to evaluate this question is a sprint burndown chart. The tool is a graphical representation of the amount of work remaining in a sprint compared to the time left in which to complete it. Sprint burndowns can be an indication of progress, helping alert the Scrum team to the potential for missing the sprint commitment.

Agile Tip

Sprint burndowns are primarily a tool for the Scrum Inner circle to monitor the health of the sprint. They are less useful for other stakeholders and may even be misinterpreted.

The time remaining in the sprint is represented by the x-axis, the units often being the number of days of the sprint. The amount of work remaining is represented by the y-axis. The units of the work remaining can be different, depending on what would be most helpful for the team to track. They may prefer to express remaining work in hours, number of tasks, or some kind of relative estimation measure, such as story points. Regardless of units used, if the sprint burndown is updated every day, it can be a useful tool for assessing the likelihood of achieving the sprint commitment.

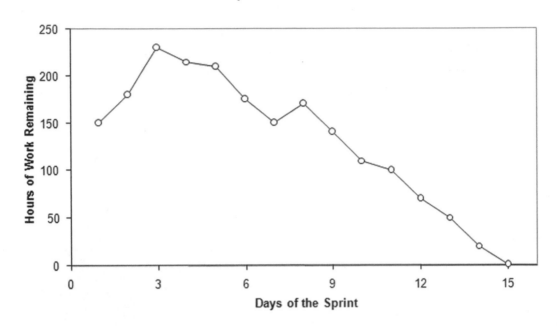

At a higher level, there is also often a need to understand the progress of not just a given sprint but also of the whole project or release. A release burndown chart is a useful tool for such issues. The layout is similar—measuring the amount of work to do versus the time in which to do it. But the difference is the graph measures this data over the course of the entire release. The x-axis of the sprint burndown chart denotes time expressed as the individual sprints themselves. The y-axis represents all the work remaining in the project or release. As each new sprint starts, the graph is updated to show two key data: the amount of work from the original backlog that is still remaining and any new work the Product Owner has added. Tracking the average rate of change of these two factors across sprints gives a good indication of when the project will be done.

The product backlog and sprint backlog, along with the burndown charts, are the primary Scrum artifacts. As you can see, it is a short list. Teams may find other documents will be necessary for projects in their organizations, and those additional requirements can certainly be added. But many teams find, with the added transparency and emphasis on regular communication, that their need for documentation greatly reduces.

Scrum as a Pathway

As you can see, the mechanics of Scrum are quite simple. But achieving mastery at anything takes a bit more effort beyond learning the basics. As companies progress through the learning curve with agile, their old habits and lack of experience with the new approach mean problems crop up. In the next section, we'll learn where problems typically occur and how to fix them. Rome wasn't built in a day. Even in the best, most agile organizations I work with, there are problems. There are teams that do well and teams that struggle. It has been said that an agile approach is not a methodology, but a pathway. Rather than trying to achieve some perfect end state, an agile organization should focus on continuous improvement. With a little patience and persistence, your organization can get started on the pathway and reap many of the benefits that agile has to offer.

Part Two

Diagnosing the Problems

This book is about identifying and fixing problems. So it will be most useful to you if your organization has at least attempted to do projects using an agile approach. Until you try agile, all problems exist in the realm of theory. So if you are still in the stage of thinking about doing agile, use the information from Part One to get started on a pilot project as soon as possible. Don't be like one of my clients that sent dozens of employees to my training courses over a two-year period but never actually got around to doing a single agile project! If you haven't already, get started today.

If you are already using an agile project management approach like Scrum for some of your projects, you have, no doubt, encountered some impediments. "Impediment" is a word that has a special meaning in Scrum. An impediment is a process or condition that exists in your organization today that is not in its best long-term interests. Sound pretty vague? That's on purpose. It's vague because impediments can be small and annoying or they can be huge and debilitating. But regardless of the impact, what all impediments have in common is that they interfere with your company's ability to deliver value.

Impediments	
Small and Annoying	Huge and Debilitating
"The Scrum team room is always too hot—we're falling asleep after lunch!"	"Next month's release has already been announced by marketing, and we have over two hundred level-one bugs plus more new features to deliver!"

Agile Tip

An impediment is a process or condition that exists in the organization that is not in its best long-term interest. The Scrum process will raise impediments, which can then be dealt with as the organization sees fit.

When you are new to agile, you tend to discover a lot of impediments—so much so that it can seem as though all you have are impediments and nothing that works right! Of course, that isn't true. But it is important in the early days not to let yourself get discouraged.

As you go through each area of focus in this section, you may find you have identifiable problems in all of them. But if you try to fix all these issues at once, it will be overwhelming. I call this tendency trying to "create world peace"—you put all your problems together in one giant mass that is so complex the only answer becomes "you can't get there from here."

Instead, take the opposite approach. Try to identify and focus on only your most pressing problems. These might be the ones that are affecting the largest number of teams. Or they might be the issues that, if fixed, would give the biggest impact to the bottom line of your business. However you measure it, make an active choice on which problems you will tackle first. This will help you use your limited time and resources in the best way.

You will also notice that in this section we talk predominantly about agile in terms of using Scrum. As mentioned before, Scrum is far and away the most popular agile framework in use today. It is possible to take a more freeform approach and use some of the agile principles (for example, an empirical approach, defined roles, and frequent inspect-and-adapt points). But I often find that organizations that do this end up subconsciously picking the parts of agile that they feel are easy to do and skip the parts that, while harder, would yield great benefit. At the same time, they often skip over removing their thorniest impediments, finding that too hard, and instead choose to work around them. This unpleasant combination often gives the worst of all worlds: organizations go through the pain of trying to make a change to agile but don't take enough active steps in the right direction to achieve good, measureable results. Scrum was created and has evolved based on experiences from all kinds of organizations, all over the world. One of my clients, a senior manager at a large technology organization, says this: "I know I am not smarter than Scrum. As soon as I find myself trying to go around the framework or add something new into it, I know I am usually on the wrong path."

My advice to you is to adopt Scrum as your agile project management framework, at least in the beginning of your agile transformation. Later, if you feel you want to try a different framework or to create a hybrid of your own, you can at least do that from a position of experience. The benefits your company can get from doing Scrum well will astound you. Let's start with that, and you can deliver world peace later.

Week 1 – Roles

In Week 1 we'll learn how to effectively fill each of the Scrum roles. We'll also learn the part stakeholders play in the Scrum process and how they can be important and helpful contributors to the overall project success.

Does this sound familiar?

1. Our teams don't like to make commitments. When they do finally commit, they "sandbag" and only commit to a small amount of work.

2. We have team members who are very "anti-Scrum" and their attitude is affecting the rest of the group.

3. Our Product Owner won't prioritize requirements—he says they are all important.

4. We have a very small team so the ScrumMaster and Product Owner roles are filled by one person.

5. Our ScrumMaster tells the team how much to commit to and also how to do the actual work.

6. The person in the ScrumMaster role also happens to be the team's manager.

7. Some of the stakeholders disagree with the priorities set by the Product Owner. Now the team is not sure whom they should listen to.

8. Our Product Owner is never available when we have questions or need clarification on requirements.

9. Our management says they want us to do Scrum—until there is pressure from a client to hit a hard delivery date. Then it is back to "hurry up and get it done!" and seventy-hour weeks.

10. Sometimes our Product Owner accepts a requirement as done but the stakeholders disagree.

Problems with the Scrum roles come, in general, in two areas: inside the Scrum inner circle, meaning the Scrum team, Product Owner, and Scrum-Master; and from outside, meaning stakeholders and management. Even if your organization is enthusiastic about Scrum, problems with roles are common. People have a set of habits, of skills they have developed to do their work in the current environment. Now you are asking them to change those habits. Even if the desire to do so is there, in practice, it can take some time to let old behaviors go. The key is recognizing when a role is being compromised and taking the steps necessary to move that person towards more productive behaviors. Of course, confusion about the Scrum roles can come in many forms, but there is a common cast of characters that show up when problems arise. Let's meet them.

The Scrum Team

A Scrum team is in the business of making and meeting commitments. When they can do that, their Product Owner and, indeed, the whole organization is usually very happy. So any behaviors that interfere with a Scrum team's ability to deliver what they said they would deliver need to be changed. When new Scrum teams are struggling to deliver value, chances are you will see these patterns:

The Sheep

The Problem

The Sheep are Scrum teams that do not self-manage. They do not like to take responsibility. Rather, they will look to the ScrumMaster, Product Owner, or even outside parties to tell them what to do. They tend to sit passively in sprint-planning meetings, letting the ScrumMaster and Product Owner do most of the talking. Their daily Scrums often feel like status updates, rather than a true coordination of work. They tend to report their progress to the ScrumMaster and also ask that person questions, like, "What should I work on now?" Sheep can easily be intimidated by a Product Owner's demands and may end up committing to far more work than they know they can deliver. "He said we had to commit to all ten user stories!" is a common refrain among Sheep. Or, by contrast, they may "sandbag," meaning make ridiculously low commitments, in an effort to protect themselves from being pushed to work at an unachievably high pace. Sheep teams are also easily distracted by stakeholder requests, even if they are in direct conflict with what the Product Owner has asked for. In summary, Sheep do not take ownership of their part of the Scrum process. Instead, they look everywhere but inside themselves and the team for guidance, protection, and direction.

Why This Happens

Some people think a Sheep team is lazy, but that is rarely the case. Instead, people on Sheep teams have often had self-management beaten out of them. In subtle and not-so-subtle ways, they have often been discouraged from taking initiative and instead told, "Just do what you are asked, nothing more or less. Don't veer off the path." Sheep teams have often spent time working in organizations that have very directive management, where employees who do what they are told are rewarded and those who display independent thought are not.

Some Sheep teams are made up of individuals who are junior-level staff. When Product Owners, ScrumMasters, and stakeholders are more senior-level people, the team's reaction to their requests can be to instantly defer to all suggestions and ideas. Their ScrumMaster makes an innocent comment like, "Have you thought of doing it this way?" and Sheep teams hear a directive: "Do it this way." Their inexperience and lack of confidence holds them back from taking a more active role in decision-making for their project.

Whatever the source of their unwillingness to self-manage, the point is the Sheep team's focus has veered away from what will most benefit the project and instead has fixed on what actions will keep anyone from being disappointed or angry with them. In their minds, they are trying to survive in a hostile environment, and anything they can do to protect themselves from the world and its demands is a good and necessary thing.

The Fix

Scrum teams *must* self-manage. The initiative, creativity, and commitment a good self-managed team shows is the engine that makes all agile development work. Without that level of ownership, it is impossible to truly reap the benefits of Scrum or any other agile framework.

So how do you turn fearful Sheep into a group of confident self-managers? Three primary things are needed for this. First, you need to create an environment where it is safe for them to self-manage. Second, you need to help the team believe it is truly safe for them to self-manage. And last, you have to wean them off the old behaviors and teach them new ones that will serve them better.

To create an environment safe for self-management, some education is required. Product Owners need to understand that the team now may push back on requests. They may not commit to everything he wants. And this is a good thing. Help your Product Owner realize that pressuring people so much that they feel compelled to essentially lie to him (saying, "Ok, we will get all ten of those requirements done this sprint" while thinking, "There is no way we can deliver all those requirements!") ultimately doesn't help anyone, least of all the Product Owner himself. Good Scrum teams know they have a responsibility to give the Product Owner the information he needs to make good business decisions. Sometimes teams have to say no, but if they are doing it from a position of honesty and a basis in fact, this is ultimately much more useful to the Product Owner.

Likewise, your management needs to learn how to treat Scrum teams in order to encourage them to self-manage. People need to be free from the fear of punishment for making mistakes. They need to know their management understands that, to come up with creative solutions, it is necessary to try some things that ultimately will not work out. And management needs to understand that pushing a team to work beyond its sustainable pace, the rate at which historical evidence shows they can create quality work, reduces quality and, ultimately, does not serve the organization's best interests.

Interestingly, even when Product Owners, stakeholders, and management adopt these new beliefs, there is often a fair amount of work required to help a team actually believe it is OK for them to self-manage. Like lab rats that have been zapped one too many times by a researcher, they will tend to cling to old habits simply out of comfort. What can help with this are some very frank and honest statements from your management and Product Owner. Just having these people publicly admit there has been a problem in the past—that *they* have been a problem in the past—can go a long way towards building trust in the team. And some teams will need to hear the message repeatedly. I once had a private-course participant say to me, "Our managers will never let us make the change you are proposing." When I explained that it was his managers that wanted the change, he still said it wouldn't work. It wasn't until his manager, who was also in the class, spoke up and said, "Listen, I am your manager, and I am telling you I will support you in making this change. I want you to do it," that the participant could finally let himself believe my suggestions might work.

The final step in getting a team to self-manage is to remove all crutches. Get them to stand on their own feet and make decisions. ScrumMasters should watch for team members treating them like managers: "I finished my task. What should I do next?" My favorite response to this question is, "I don't know. What do you think you should do next?" By refusing to manage the team, you help them build the skills they need to manage themselves.

Product Owners can likewise help a team make good commitments. Just checking in with a statement like, "So you are committing to five user stories. Do you have good confidence you can deliver those?" is a double-check on the team's level of belief in their commitments. An answer like, "Well, we will give it a try," can be a sign they still are making commitments based on what the Product Owner wants, not what the team knows they can deliver.

The Bad Apples

The Problem

You know the Bad Apples. They are the ones that are sure "this Scrum thing" is a waste of time. They may overtly or covertly try to thwart the process at every turn. They "forget" meetings, like the daily Scrum, and can often be found in the sprint-planning meeting checking messages on their phone, only looking up to voice an occasional objection as to why something won't work. If they had their way, the team would stop doing Scrum and go back to the old way of doing things. Not coincidentally, the old way was usually a pretty nice set-up for them, despite the fact the organization found it less useful.

> ## Agile Tip
>
> Self-managing teams are the cornerstone of all agile product development. The principle behind this approach says the creativity and effectiveness of the group will be better than any one person's ideas. With self-managed teams, the whole is greater than the sum of the parts.

Why This Happens

Bad Apples come in two forms. First, there are the people who really do have honest questions about how Scrum works. In their minds, they see problems with Scrum fitting into the organization. The great thing about this type of Bad Apple is that, if you can answer those questions, you can win them over. These people can become some of your greatest supporters if, in their minds, they can get their nagging questions answered.

The other kind of Bad Apple is much more dangerous. These are people who dislike Scrum because they are threatened by it. For example, they may be happy to cruise along, working at 60-percent effort, and chafe against the idea of having to make commitments. Or they may be information hoarders, those who have specialized knowledge and get their power in the organization by keeping their knowledge close to them, doling it out stingily like Scrooge in the smallest bits possible and only when absolutely necessary. There is also a special kind of Bad Apple called a Rock Star. The Rock Star lives in a universe where he is the center around which everything and everyone else should revolve. He is often technically brilliant but will work strictly on this own terms. He prefers to work alone and often takes a "my way or the highway" approach to design, mercilessly belittling anyone who dares to disagree with him.

The Fix

Bad Apples are especially dangerous when an organization is just getting started with Scrum. Their negative attitude can poison the whole team and kill a Scrum pilot effort before it ever gets off the ground. One way to avoid having Bad Apples is to allow a Scrum team to self-select. By this, I mean choose people for the team who want to be there, people who have expressed an interest in Scrum and want to try it. This is your best chance at building a team of people with the right attitude.

When you feel that a team member might be exhibiting Bad-Apple behavior because he has unanswered questions, consider a conversation in private to discuss them. See if you can find out what is bothering him and provide some answers. Help him understand that adopting Scrum is a learning process. There will be some questions that will need to be answered over time through the experience of trying things and seeing the result. This is the nature of an empirical approach. Sometimes people who deal with the world from an intellectual stance feel a need to have all the answers up front before they can support a solution. But Scrum is designed to deal with uncertainty. So helping this kind of Bad Apple see that it is normal to not have all the answers in the first sprints of a Scrum project is normal and natural.

Bad Apples with valid concerns can often be won over gradually to Scrum. But Rock Stars and other people who are threatened by Scrum cannot. Instead, they must be removed from the team. Their negative attitude will poison a team, dragging it down. Their protests that Scrum will not work end up becoming a self-fulfilling prophecy. Ultimately, if the entire organization moves towards Scrum, these Bad Apples may choose to leave the company. In their minds, they would rather leave the organization than change their ways and work as part of a self-managed, self-organizing team.

The Class System

The Problem

Class-system teams appear in companies that have a strong implied or defined hierarchy. In such an organization, team members are strictly ranked according to importance. And that level of importance determines what kinds of decisions that person can make. You know you have a class system when you see behaviors like senior engineers being the only ones who can do estimates. They, in turn, tell the junior engineers how long their work "should" take. Another characteristic of a class system is that, even when two people have the same title, one person is the "chosen one" and therefore is listened to more often. Finally, one of the worst things about a Class-system team is that the members get pigeon-holed. They started at the organization doing a certain kind of work, and somewhere along the way, it is assumed that is all they can do. People doing creative technical work need to learn and grow. They need an opportunity to face new challenges. But the Class-system team thwarts this, limiting both their professional and their personal growth.

> **Agile Tip**
>
> Some employees may never adapt to working in the Scrum framework. It is not unusual for organizations that move to Scrum to have a small amount of staff turnover because of this.

Why This Happens

Class Systems may start out with good intentions. They have people with expert knowledge in an area, so naturally, when there are questions, people turn to these people for answers. But the problem occurs when this person remains the only one with this knowledge. When no effort is made to cross-train or to otherwise spread knowledge, this person becomes, in effect, a gate-keeper. Worse, anyone else asked to learn this work is not going to be motivated. She knows people will not take her answers seriously but, instead, will go around her to the recognized expert. This is an incredibly demotivating situation. Often being the "second tier" person in a job role makes the person simply give up, putting out as little effort as possible to do the job, having learned helplessness.

Sometimes the Class System develops due to favoritism and friendships. Managers find themselves trusting one employee more than others because that person is a friend. An "old boys' network" can develop, whether intended or not, that effectively excludes other employees. For those in the excluded group, no behavior they exhibit at work can gain them access to the favored group because being part of that group is not based on any work-related criteria.

The Fix

Class Systems are anathema to Scrum. While it is acknowledged that team members have different skills and experience levels, they are, nevertheless, still equal. Everyone on a team has a voice and is expected to use it. So Class-system teams should use practices that help every team member have an equal voice. One such practice that can be used to help with estimation is planning poker. There are special card decks made for planning poker. But you can also simply use the any five cards from a regular card deck. When teams are ready to estimate a given requirement, each person has his planning-poker deck ready. Each person on the team selects the card he thinks reflects the level of effort required to complete the requirement and places the card face down, in front of him. Then, together, all team members turn over their cards. Everyone showing his card at once allows each team member to be honest and avoid undue influence from others.

Another technique Class-system teams can use to encourage equality is silent writing. This is particularly useful during a sprint retrospective, when the team will discuss what did and did not go well during the sprint. Teams with class issues find it can be useful to start their retrospectives with a period of silent writing where team members put their comments on individual Post-its. These Post-its are then grouped into general categories of "went well" and "needs work." Giving team members the freedom to write rather than speak can improve their willingness to take chances, express their real thoughts, and be honest.

How well do your teams self-manage?

Try not to think of the answer to the question above as black or white but rather on a continuum. Teams that display any of the characteristics in this section will need active facilitation by a ScrumMaster to learn other more productive behaviors. But even that assistance should be temporary. Ultimately, the team must learn to rely on each other, as equals and partners, to determine how best to meet the commitments that they, as a group, have made. Try to instill a little more independence and sense of ownership in them each day. Doing so will ensure they gradually improve and continually feel they have more control and contribution over the work they do.

The Product Owner

In early Scrum literature, the Product Owner is sometimes rather unkindly referred to as the "single wringable neck." What this unflattering nickname tries to convey is the importance of the job. This is the person who will set the overall direction of the product, decide what does and doesn't make it into the feature set, and determine the return on investment for the entire project. If a Scrum team builds a technically sound product and it doesn't meet the needs of the organization, there truly is one person to blame: the Product Owner.

Having a good Product Owner is crucial to the success of the Scrum project. But unfortunately, is it one of the most common areas in which organizations have problems. Part of the problem stems from the fact that Product

Owners are often the last people in the company to be sent to training. They get a hasty introduction to Scrum and a rough overview of their responsibilities, and then they are thrown into their first project. Not surprisingly, they often fail. Simply getting your Product Owners to a Scrum certification course can go a long way towards helping with the knowledge gap.

But even after training, some Product Owners are not successful. When Product Owners have received adequate training and are still not performing well in the role, you may see these behaviors:

The Bully

The Problem

The Bully browbeats the team. He won't take no for an answer. He comes into the sprint-planning meeting ready to tell the team the requirements to which they "must" commit. He argues with the team on estimates and says things like, "It can't take that long—it's just a little change!" Sometimes the Bully will "help" the team by doing estimates for them. In the daily Scrum, he may pepper them with questions, wanting to know why this or that was not finished. In short, he behaves like a tyrant. The Bully Product Owner is particularly bad in combination with a Sheep team. In such situations, the team is cowed into submission and rendered ineffective. They commit to work they know they will not be able to finish and leave their Product Owner constantly disappointed and complaining loudly to anyone who will listen, "You can't count on this team at all."

Why This Happens

One way this situation can develop is when the Product Owner is also the manager of the team. In such cases, the Bully may feel it is not only his right but also his duty to push the team. It is nearly always a terrible idea to choose a team's manager as their Product Owner. The problem is you have two variables at play—the manager's ability to control his own behavior and the team's willingness to trust him. You have to count on the Product Owner to rein in the bossing and to respect a team's decisions about commitments, technical approach, and other decisions that they own. But let's say the Product Owner manages to do this. He tells the team, "Hey, when it comes to our Scrum project, I am not your manager. I am your Product Owner." Even then, the team has to believe him. They have to trust that he is not making negative mental notes on their annual review every time they say they cannot commit a product backlog item or admit they are having a problem.

Another way the Bully develops is when the person in that role believes that no work will get done unless he pushes. This kind of Bully honestly believes all the nagging, threatening, and cajoling is directly responsible for any progress being made. Like an overbearing parent, this kind of Bully feels the best way to reduce risk is to micromanage every aspect of each team member's life.

The Fix

The Bully must be reined in. His forceful approach will crush a fledgling team's efforts at self-management. And, in the beginning at least, it often falls to the ScrumMaster to do the reining. In the earliest days of Scrum, the ScrumMaster role was often primarily seen as that of a protector to the team, keeping the Product Owner and stakeholders at bay so the team could work uninterrupted. This is the action required now. The ScrumMaster must help the Bully know when his behavior has crossed the line. It is reasonable for a Product Owner to want as much productivity from a team as possible. It is not, however, reasonable that he should demand the impossible. If a Scrum team makes a commitment that is less than the Product Owner hoped, he certainly has the right to question them about it. But he must do so in a respectful way and not as part of a personal attack. And if the team confirms that, in fact, they cannot take on any more work, that must be the end of the discussion. Period.

Because the ScrumMaster will often have to keep the Product Owner's zeal for productivity in check, it is important that these two roles are filled by individuals who are well matched in temperament. A bombastic Product Owner prone to yelling needs an equally forceful ScrumMaster to balance his approach. Be aware that some Bullies come disguised as Pleaders—a Product Owner who talks a team into committing to too much not by threats but by begging. They say things like, "Oh pleeeeease! I really need these five extra features by next sprint!" In these cases, a ScrumMaster must step in before the team can be seduced and ensure the Pleader doesn't set the sprint up for failure. In all cases, the ScrumMaster can help reduce the Bully's impact by stepping in when necessary to bolster the team's message.

The Wimp

The Problem

If the Bully goes through the Scrum world trying to personally orchestrate everything around him, the Wimp is just the opposite. The Wimp hates making decisions. He probably doesn't enjoy the Product Owner role very much because it seems people are always asking him to make hard choices, which leaves him wringing his hands in anxiety. To ease these fears, he leans on others. Under the guise of gaining consensus, he basically turns over his decision-making role to others. Teams know they have a Wimp Product Owner when the product backlog changes wildly from sprint to sprint for no visible or logical reason. What items have the highest priority are based on who is influencing him at the time.

The Wimp can even be over-influenced by the team. When team members insist the backlog be ordered in a certain way (usually to make life easier for them), the Wimp instantly gives in. He doesn't ask for clarification or help understanding the reasoning behind this—he simply puts his backlog in the order the team tells him. A Wimp Product Owner is a particularly bad combination with a Bad Apple team, especially if that team has one or more Rock Stars. The Rock Star knows he can intimidate the Wimp into doing things his way. He knows this will happen because the Wimp is looking for any excuse to surrender decision-making to someone else. The product backlog produced by a Rock Star/Wimp personality combination often looks not like a list of business requirements but more like a technical specification. The items are written from a technical perspective and arranged not to deliver the most business value but to make the Rock Star's life easier.

Why This Happens

The Wimp Product Owner is often the wrong person for the job. Someone who dislikes making decisions is never truly going to be comfortable in the Product Owner role. The single most important thing a Product Owner must prepare himself for in his role is occasionally making people unhappy. The Product Owner is constantly making hard decisions about business value.

This means that sometimes he has to make choices that benefit the overall good of the company but disappoint a particular stakeholder. This is par for the course in a Product Owner's life. So someone who pales at the thought of having to do that will find it very difficult to be happy, much less successful, in the role.

Occasionally a Wimp simply doesn't realize, when he is new to Scrum, that he has the right to say no to anyone. In such cases, education can improve this person's effectiveness. The ScrumMaster can encourage him to question the team, ensuring that the statement, "We have to do it this way," doesn't really mean "It would be easiest for the technical team if we did it this way." It can be particularly helpful for a ScrumMaster to help a Product Owner in this way when that person has a non-technical background. The team should be able to explain—in layman's terms, not tech-speak—their reasoning and also other options for the Product Owner to consider.

A Wimp may also be carrying habits over from a past role. Business analysts—the people in many organizations charged with gathering and writing requirements—often struggle in the role of Product Owner for this very reason. At first, they seem like a natural choice—someone who already has connections with the stakeholders and knows how to document requirements effectively. But former business analysts quickly learn that gathering and documenting a stakeholder's request is a very different thing from telling that stakeholder he cannot have something. Many business analysts cannot make the transition. They continue to build their backlogs like requirements documents, adding every whim and desire the stakeholders request with no thought to business value or return on investment.

The Fix

The Wimp needs both support and tough love from his ScrumMaster. He must learn that the nature of a Product Owner's life is making decisions. There is no escape from that fact. So instead of spending his energy trying to avoid this responsibility, the Wimp must, instead, focus on gathering the information he needs to make the best, most well-informed decisions possible.

The ScrumMaster can support a weak Product Owner by helping him ask the questions he might be thinking but is unsure about voicing. Reminding a Scrum team to explain issues in layman's terms to a non-technical Product

Owner is another way to help. The ScrumMaster can also watch for the Product Owner's power being usurped by management. The leaders of an organization are an important stakeholder group. The Product Owner must be very aware of their concerns. But when management constantly second-guesses a Product Owner, especially in front of the team and other stakeholders, they are setting that person up for failure. Like a Sheep team, the Wimp Product Owner learns his decisions and boundaries are not respected, so there is no point in taking the initiative to have them at all.

Ultimately, you must help a Wimp realize that he has to make decisions. If he will not or cannot decide, he is not fulfilling the Product Owner role. The Wimp needs to toughen up. He needs to realize that life (at least, a Product Owner's life) is not a popularity contest. It is about making hard decisions about how to best use limited time and resources. When he starts to see that the organization is counting on him to do this, a Wimp may surprise everyone with his newfound confidence and decisiveness.

The Disappearing Act

The Problem

Perhaps the most frustrating type of Product Owner, at least from the perspective of the Scrum team, is the Disappearing Act. As the name implies, the Disappearing Act is never there. He rarely attends a daily Scrum and sometimes cannot even be counted on to show up for sprint-planning meetings. He is not available to give the team direction or answer their questions. He does not maintain the product backlog and constantly needs help from the ScrumMaster and others to do this. The Disappearing Act may meet with stakeholders and learn about requirements, but somehow, the results of these meetings never seem to get translated into product-backlog items. In short, the Disappearing Act is not really fulfilling the role of Product Owner.

Why This Happens

The Disappearing Act is often thrust into the role of Product Owner without truly understanding what will be expected of him. Sometimes, in their enthusiasm to get someone—anyone—to be a Product Owner, teams and ScrumMasters will consciously or unconsciously minimize the amount of work expected from this individual. They will say something like, "You'll give us your requirements, just as you do now. You just need to put them into a prioritized list." Left out of this description is the time it takes to consider all the factors that go into that prioritization. The Disappearing Act tries to fit being a Product Owner in his spare time. He thinks of the role as an extra thing, on the side, that he will do when and if time is available after all his "real" work is done.

The Fix

The Disappearing Act has rarely received any training in Scrum. Most likely, he got a hasty explanation from the team or ScrumMaster about what will be expected from him. If, instead, he had attended one of the certified Scrum trainings, he would have a much better idea of the importance of the Product Owner role. So one of the best things you can do for a Disappearing Act is to make sure he gets proper training in Scrum. A ten-minute chat and tossing a book on his desk (even this book!) is not going to cut it for the individual who must guide the overall vision of the product.

The Disappearing Act may also be struggling to fulfill the Product Owner role because he is simply being asked to do too much. In such cases, educating his management is important. Like Product Owners, managers are often educated in Scrum as an afterthought. Because of this, they do not understand the amount of time required to fulfill this important Scrum role. Helping managers understand the amount of time required to be a good Product Owner can be the first step to helping the Disappearing Act get the time he needs to do this work.

But if this Product Owner has received training and is still missing in action, you have a serious problem. Scrum projects rarely succeed without someone at the helm making the tough choices about priority. It will usually fall to the ScrumMaster to have a frank and honest discussion with the Disappearing Act to help him understand how his lack of availability is hurting the project. One thing that can help this kind of Product Owner is a formal communication plan. Ask your Product Owner, "If we need a decision immediately and we can't reach you, what should we do?" Be sure to set up the communication plan *before* you need it. Having this fallback can help a busy Product Owner have the confidence that work is progressing according to his goals, even when he cannot be there.

If none of these efforts seem to help, you may have the wrong person in the Product Owner role. This means working with management to find someone better suited for the job. But what you should definitely not do is let the ScrumMaster or team take on the role of Product Owner. As soon as these people start making Product-owner-type decisions about priority and doneness, you have lost an important checks-and-balances role. The three Scrum roles exist for a reason, to use different responsibilities and controls to move towards an overall common goal. When one of these roles is effectively missing, the whole project will suffer.

ScrumMaster

Though a ScrumMaster is often described as a facilitator, in truth there is much more to the role. True, a large portion of a ScrumMaster's time will be spent coaching and helping both the Scrum team and Product Owner. In this way, the ScrumMaster guides the Scrum process itself. But there is another larger piece to the role. The ScrumMaster is the person most likely to spread Scrum throughout the organization. She works with management to remove impediments. She may provide reporting from the Scrum project. She helps outside groups understand how the Scrum team's work may affect them. Ultimately, a ScrumMaster may evolve into the role of an internal agile coach, helping to drive organizational change. It is sometimes said that the ScrumMaster's role is to socialize Scrum. This means she helps everyone in the organization learn how to use Scrum to further the overall goals of the company.

While the ScrumMaster is clearly a leadership role in Scrum, it is also a role that has no traditional authority. This means ScrumMasters do not manage their Scrum teams or Product Owner or anyone else, for that matter. They are, instead, servant leaders. A good ScrumMaster uses observations and questions not to tell a team what to do but to lead a team to discovering for themselves what to do.

Problems can occur in the ScrumMaster's role when the people fulfilling the role bring old behaviors and working patterns with them into the job. ScrumMasters may have strong personalities, and there is nothing wrong with that—unless the behaviors associated with their personality impair the Scrum process. When that happens, you may encounter these problems:

The Master of Disguise

The Problem

The Master of Disguise brings all the skills from her old job as a project manager into her new job as ScrumMaster. She sees herself as personally responsible for the overall success or failure of the project. Because of this, she will take a highly directive role in her Scrum projects. Interchanges between her and the team are directed almost exclusively by her. She asks them questions—they answer. She raises concerns about their ability to meet their commitment—they must defend themselves. If she feels a team is making poor decisions, she will step in and make other decisions for them. She takes a similar approach with the Product Owner, treating him like a difficult customer that needs to be managed. She may tell the Product Owner what he can and cannot put on the Product Backlog and even what order it should be in. And the Master of Disguise feels it is her duty—not the Product Owner's—to bring stakeholders' concerns to the team. She will let them know what management expects from them and will in no way act as a filter or protect them as a ScrumMaster should. In short, the Master of Disguise is only pretending to be a ScrumMaster. In reality, she is still—in her behavior, thoughts, and actions—a project manager.

Why This Happens

Sometimes the Master of Disguise has been set up to fail by her company. Organizations that do Scrum at a superficial level often take existing project roles and simply paste on a new Scrum title, without ever considering how the nature of the job must change. This is especially true for project managers. Organizations may think project managers and ScrumMasters are basically the same and consider themselves to be doing Scrum when they replace one job title with the other. What they do not realize is that the responsibilities for the two roles are not only different but they are also in direct conflict with one another. A project manager has overarching responsibility for the success of the project. A ScrumMaster does not. She is not responsible for ensuring the work promised in a sprint is delivered—that is the team's responsibility. Nor is she responsible for ensuring the right features and functionality are delivered—that belongs to the Product Owner. Instead, the ScrumMaster is responsible for the process itself. Unlike a project manager, she must take a distinctly neutral role in these matters to encourage the other parties—the Scrum team and Product Owner—to take responsibility in their respective areas.

Even if her organization provides support in allowing a ScrumMaster to set aside her project-management duties, she may find the hardest battle is with herself and her own habits. Good project managers often have very directive personalities. They can come into a project, assess the situation, and quickly take control. ScrumMasters, on the other hand, do not seek to control projects. Instead, they try to help Product Owners and Scrum teams be successful in their roles such that the project controls itself. Learning these new behaviors can be hard. The Master of Disguise often feels the world is a safer place with her in charge, and letting go of these ideas can produce a good deal of discomfort.

The Fix

The first step in helping a Master of Disguise is making sure the organization understands her role has now changed. She cannot be judged by the same standard as when she was a project manager. Ideally, this can be handled by working with the human resources department to create new job descriptions for all the Scrum roles. Taking this action shows an acknowledgement of the fact that these jobs are different from what has been done in the past.

If creating new job descriptions is too daunting early in a Scrum adoption, minimally, a ScrumMaster's annual goals and objectives must be changed. The approach to the annual review process varies from company to company. In general, there tend to be some overarching goals that must be included. But within those categories, most companies allow the manager and employee a fair amount of freedom to decide how those goals can be met. This is the opportunity needed to work in more Scrum-like goals for the ScrumMaster. She should be judged not on her ability to direct and control the team but, instead, on her efforts to support them in self-management. She should be encouraged to coach and support the Product Owner. And she should have goals around raising—and helping management evaluate—organizational impediments. Taking these steps to demonstrate the ScrumMaster will not be judged as a product manager will help ensure a Master of Disguise is not still acting as one.

If the organization supports her in the new role and the Master of Disguise still acts in a very directive and controlling way, she must be made aware her own behavior, thoughts, and attitudes must change. Periodically having another ScrumMaster sit in on Scrum meetings can be a checkpoint for a ScrumMaster to alert her to when her behaviors tend to take on an "It's all up to me!" theme. It is hard for us to see our own behavior patterns. Having a neutral set of eyes can sometimes help us see where we fall short and show us how we might be more effective.

Ultimately, one of the best techniques for redirecting the behavior of a Master of Disguise is a shift in focus. This kind of ScrumMaster must take her ability to drive people and work and, instead, use it to drive organizational change. It is often these strong personalities—former managers and project managers—that become key catalysts in an agile transformation. They are not afraid to "lay it on the line." They do not sugar-coat problems. It is often this kind of ScrumMaster who will say what everyone in the room is thinking but is too intimidated to say out loud. When a Master of Disguise can make this shift in her behavior, she becomes a key contributor to forging the path her organization will take to agility.

The Juggler

The Problem

Unlike the Master of Disguise, who sees her involvement in projects as pivotal to their success, the Juggler sees the ScrumMaster role as a primarily administrative one. If asked to describe what a ScrumMaster does, what the role must produce, she would say something like, "Set up and facilitate the Scrum meetings and help out if any impediments come up." She would describe the role as something that takes, on average, a few minutes a day. The Juggler has this limited view of the ScrumMaster role in mind when she plans her work. Consequently, she takes on much more outside work than she should. She may take on the ScrumMaster's role for five or six teams. She may choose to be a ScrumMaster and also a Scrum team member. Or she may consider ScrumMastering to be something she can fit in her spare time while continuing do her old job. In each case, the Juggler's expectations about the amount of effort required to do the ScrumMaster's role means she really fulfills it only at a superficial level. Because she has not budgeted the time for it, she cannot tackle the deeper issues. She cannot help remove impediments, spread Scrum throughout the organization, or guide the overall agile transformation because she never has the time to delve into these issues in any depth.

Why This Happens

The Juggler lacks a full understanding of the ScrumMaster's role. It is true that administrative tasks, like setting up the Scrum meetings, are part of the job. But they are far and away the smallest part. Much more time-consuming is helping the organization change. It is often the ScrumMaster that has the vision of what his or her company might be like when the benefits of Scrum are fully realized. Helping others see this vision and ultimately make it a reality is the most complex part of what it means to be a ScrumMaster.

This disconnect may occur because the organization also believes being a ScrumMaster is an administrative job. This can often happen when a company simply stamps the title "ScrumMaster" on its project managers. Believing the job to be status reporting and a once-a-week check-in with the team, the organization piles work on the Juggler. In such cases, this kind of ScrumMaster has no time to perform the full scope of her job. She limits herself, therefore, to the parts that can be most easily defined: the Scrum meetings. A team with a Juggler ScrumMaster lives in constant frustration with impediments because they can get no help in resolving them. Or the team may take on the work of resolving impediments themselves, thereby taking away from the time they have to meet commitments.

Another way the Juggler develops is when she truly does not understand the breadth of the ScrumMaster's role. She may lack a complete understanding of what she is expected to do on a day-to-day basis. She may not realize that it is her job to help remove organizational impediments, coach the Product Owner, and help the organization change. Either she has been told or she assumes that being a ScrumMaster means setting up meetings, and she has scheduled her work accordingly.

The Fix

The way to solve the Juggler's problem is through education. You must help this kind of ScrumMaster understand how much more attention her role requires than she is currently giving it. Managers can help with this by scheduling regular meetings to discuss organizational impediments. Having a planned time each week to review all organizational impediments, prioritize them, and discuss ways to remove them can nudge the Juggler in the direction of fulfilling her role more completely. Managers can also set ScrumMasters up for success by not giving them too much to do. Particularly for someone new to Scrum, being a ScrumMaster for one team is usually plenty.

This is particularly true when the team's Product Owner is also new to Scrum. Scrum-Masters starting new projects with completely untrained Product Owners can expect to spend as much as 50–70 percent of their time early in the project simply coaching and working with this person. These Product Owners know nothing about what the Scrum team expects from them, how to go about creating a product backlog, or what Scrum requires them to do on a daily basis. It will fall on the ScrumMaster to teach these skills.

> ## Agile Tip
>
> Former project managers can make excellent ScrumMasters. But they must remember the roles do not mix. A person can be a team's project manager or ScrumMaster, but not both.

Finally, a ScrumMaster must leave ample time in her schedule to act as a guide for organizational change. This is often the thorniest, most time-consuming part of the job. A ScrumMaster might get a request from the project management office, such as, "We'd like to revise all our current project documentation to better reflect Scrum projects, and we'd like your help." For most companies, this is not an effort that will be accomplished in a two-hour meeting. Having the time and patience to develop these new processes is where a ScrumMaster really begins to affect organizational change. After all this work is done, if she still has hours of spare time, then she can think about taking on additional teams or responsibilities.

The Enabler

The Problem

At first glance, the Enabler seems as if she is enthusiastically fulfilling her role as ScrumMaster. She actively facilitates the Scrum team, coaches the Product Owner, and works with management to remove impediments and provide project information. The problem is, in her zeal to make Scrum work well in the organization, she picks up any and all slack in the other Scrum roles. If the team regularly misses commitments, it is the Enabler, not the team itself, who explains this to management and stakeholders. She "takes the heat" for them. If they cannot make a commitment by the end of the sprint-planning meeting, she extends the meeting. If the Scrum team members are uncomfortable bringing up issues and problems in the sprint retrospective, once again, the Enabler is there to help. She lets the team avoid uncomfortable discussions by taking them on herself, often acting as a negotiator between the affected parties.

The Enabler's approach may be similar with the Product Owner. If he supposedly doesn't have time to write user stories, the Enabler is happy to step in to do it. If the Product Owner won't spend the time to work with stakeholders to understand and gather requirements, once again, the Enabler is there to pick up the slack. As a matter of fact, if the Product Owner is just so busy that he can't really be bothered to do the job at all, the Enabler becomes the de facto Product Owner, picking up all of the tasks and making all of the decisions that would normally be part of that role.

Why This Happens

The Enabler often views a Scrum project as a series of tasks rather than discrete areas of responsibility. In her mind, she may think of the total work to do in the project as a single list. It may not be obvious to her that the roles and responsibilities in Scrum are divided for a reason. So she pitches in to help others fill their roles, not realizing that she is helping to instill in them weak behaviors. The Enabler is a threat to the important checks-and-balances system of Scrum.

An Enabler often has a sense of responsibility for a project. This is another pattern commonly found in those who used to be project managers. In their minds, it is their job to fix things that go wrong. Because they are so busy fixing others' problems, they never give them the opportunities they need—sometimes through hard experiences—to learn to fix these issues themselves. A common question from an Enabler is, "But what if I let them try to fix things on their own and they fail?" The answer, of course, is that then the other party—be it a Scrum team or Product Owner—has an opportunity to learn from the experience. Once they are no longer rescued from tough situations, they quickly learn not to get themselves into these predicaments in the first place.

The Fix

The first order of business is to make the Enabler aware of her actions. This behavior pattern can often be done quite unconsciously. Work with the Enabler to help her realize that everyone on a Scrum team needs to take responsibility for his or her actions and decisions. Help her to see that, as long as she shelters a Scrum team that continually misses their commitments, they will likely never reexamine the way they are making those commitments. As long as she builds the backlog for the Product Owner, he will never put the hard thought into prioritizing it himself. The Enabler must learn that her ultimate goal is not to oversee every minute part of the Scrum process, stepping in when anything goes wrong. Rather, it is to instill the skills and sense of ownership in the Scrum team and Product Owner such that they do this themselves. Like so many in positions of leadership, a good ScrumMaster must strive to work herself out of a job. She must instill independence in the other Scrum roles such that they hardly need her at all.

Additional Roles

While the Scrum team, Product Owner, and ScrumMaster make up the Scrum inner circle, individuals outside this group also have the power to affect Scrum projects for better or worse. In general, we refer to people outside the Scrum inner circle as "stakeholders." Stakeholders are important to a Scrum project because they hold the key to knowing which features and functionalities will bring the most business value. But, compared to the Scrum inner circle, stakeholders know very little about the Scrum framework. Because of this, they may not know what are or are not helpful or appropriate ways to contribute to a Scrum project. Below we look at common problems with stakeholders, including a special kind of stakeholder that has a unique ability to wreak havoc: management.

Stakeholders

The Wish-lister

The Problem

The Wish-lister has a list of features and desires a mile long. Since these individuals rarely have to take financial responsibility for their requests, their list of must-haves includes true core functionality and also frivolous bells and whistles. It is nearly impossible to have discussions with Wish-listers about tradeoffs because, in their minds, there are no tradeoffs. Since they are not footing the bill for this extravaganza, they are not shy about asking for the moon.

Why This Happens

Wish-lister behavior often develops when the people paying for the software are not the same group that will be using it. An example of this might be call center software. Customer service representatives are the main group to use this software to help them manage customer information. So, in their minds, anything that helps with this is justifiable for inclusion in the final product. However the people paying for the software are usually the call-center management. While they also care about customer service, they know that services levels must be judged against cost. Therefore, they strive to strike a balance between including enough features in their software to meet customers' needs while still making certain the features included ultimately provide a benefit that is commensurate with their costs.

The Fix

Many of the uncomfortable conversations of a Product Owner's life take place with Wish-listers. It falls to the Product Owner to explain that, while the desires of the stakeholders are important, there will inevitably be more desires than budget. So careful consideration must be made as to which features will ultimately be included. Instead of asking Wish-listers which features are must-haves (they will say, "All of them"), the Product Owner should ask these stakeholders to explain the benefits of the feature being considered. A useful question for uncovering the business value of a potential feature is, "Help me understand the need for this feature—how do you perform this function today?" This allows the Product Owner to consider if a new feature would improve the business process sufficiently to justify its cost.

It is often useful to invite stakeholders into product-backlog grooming sessions. This can be an opportunity for the team, Product Owner, and ScrumMaster to gather requirements. But be wary of inviting too many stakeholders to any meeting. Wish-listers tend to feed off each other—"I need feature A!" "Well, I need Feature A and Feature B!" Before you know it, they will completely take over the meeting. So if you think you have Wish-lister stakeholders, be sure to invite them to backlog grooming sessions in small groups of two or three. Never let yourself—the Scrum inner circle—be outnumbered by Wish-listers or they will quickly take over and anarchy will ensue.

The Nitpicker

The Problem

The Nitpicker comes to the sprint-review meeting for the opportunity to see incremental progress on the project. And he is never satisfied. Whatever level of functionality a feature has, it is not enough for the Nitpicker. This kind of stakeholder would like to reject every feature. There is always, it seems, something that is not quite right. Nitpickers may envision the features in question should have much more functionality than they do. Or they may simply constantly change their minds. Last sprint they wanted blue—this sprint they want green. This back-and-forth on features is dangerous to a project on two fronts. First, it is discouraging to the Scrum team to constantly change and undo work. If it is for a valid business reason, they can be understanding but not so if it is due to whim. Second, every frivolous change adds costs to the project. This should—and usually does—alarm the Product Owner, who is charged with managing return on investment. A group of Nitpickers can quickly send project costs spiraling out of control.

Why This Happens

Nitpickers are often stakeholders who do not have a good understanding of Scrum. They are confused about what "done" means in Scrum. When teams and Product Owners discuss whether a feature is "done," they mean to say: does this feature provide the functionality we agreed to when we committed to deliver it in the sprint? If the answer is yes, then that feature should be accepted as done. Does that mean the feature can do everything it needs to when it is rolled out to customers? Maybe. But maybe not. For example, a Product Owner might write a requirement to build a "customer details" page, and the requirement to call it done might be "able to add first and last names, address, phone number, and email address for a customer." If that is the agreement and it has been met, the Product Owner will accept this feature as done for the sprint. But will the "customer details" page eventually have more functionality? Almost certainly. There will probably be an "edit customer information" function and perhaps the ability to "delete customer" as well. There may be a need for multiple phone numbers and multiple email addresses. And here is the part the Nitpicker does not understand: when the Product Owner desires those new functions, he will write and prioritize additional requirements describing them. Nitpickers tend to hear the term "done" and think in terms of the whole project being done. But that is not the meaning of "done" in Scrum. "Done" simply means the agreed-upon functionality for this stage of the project is in the feature and it works as promised.

The Fix

The Product Owner and ScrumMaster must show a united front against Nitpickers. They can remind them, "Yes, the other functionality you are describing is important, and it may be included in future requirements." This helps Nitpickers learn they will get what they need, just not all at once. It is helpful, when the team presents features in the sprint-review meeting, first to read the acceptance criteria. Often phrased as "Done when …," acceptance criteria describe the agreement between the Product Owner and team as to the minimum acceptable level of functionality. Doing this can help Nitpickers learn that functionality in Scrum projects is not an all-or-nothing proposition. Rather, features are enhanced and expanded in each sprint until the Product Owner deems the entire project done.

The Usurper

The Problem

The Usurper makes it his life's work to maneuver around the Product Owner to direct the Scrum team himself. In his mind, he is the one who really knows what needs to be done. Overtly or covertly, a Usurper questions the Product Owner's right to lead the project. He finds reasons to interact with the team directly, often making requests of them that are in direct conflict with the Product Owner's wishes. The Usurper may also make his pleas to management, expressing concern over the way the Product Owner is directing the team. He can even take this interference one step further, going directly to the customer. This can be especially damaging if the Usurper is someone the customers knows well and trusts. In such cases, the Product Owner will lose credibility with the customer and eventually may find everyone involved—even the ScrumMaster and Scrum team—working around him and rendering him almost useless.

> ## Agile Tip
>
> In organizations that are new to Scrum, stakeholders must often be reminded that all requirement requests must be funneled through the Product Owner. He has final say on what makes it into the product.

Why This Happens

The Usurper can develop when that person has a vested interest in having his own needs met over the Product Owner's goals. An example of when this can happen is with a salesperson. This individual's goal is to sell something to the customer. In pursuing this goal, he may ignore the Product Owner's desires for the overall project in an effort to promise something to the client that will "seal the deal." Another situation in which a Usurper can develop is when the Product Owner is new to the job. In such cases, the Usurper does not trust the Product Owner to make the right decisions. In his mind, he is still weighing whether or not the Product Owner knows what he is doing. Therefore, if any decision is suspect, the Usurper feels he is doing everyone a service if he steps in and takes control before mistakes happen. But perhaps the most dangerous Usurper of all is someone from upper management. These individuals often give the title of Product Owner to someone in name only. But the true decision making still remains firmly in their court.

Effectively, they are saying to the Product Owner, "I don't have time to do all the grunt work for this project—going to sprint-planning meetings, writing the product backlog, and so forth. So you do that. But I will keep all the decision-making power."

The Fix

There is a reason the Product Owner has final say on all requirement issues. It is because he and he alone will be held accountable for the overall product. Every Product Owner must have the ability and authority to make and stick to decisions. It is very much a "decider" role. Any behavior from stakeholders that interferes with that decision-making process will ultimately harm a Scrum project. Of course, the Product Owner should understand the concerns of all stakeholders, including management, and take them into consideration when creating and prioritizing the product backlog. But it is the nature of a Product Owner's life to have to make people unhappy. There are inevitably more wishes and desires from stakeholders than budget and time to deliver on those desires. Therefore, it is crucial a Product Owner understand the organization's most important goals so he can ensure the product backlog—and, ultimately, the project—reflects those needs.

Management—A Special Breed of Stakeholder

Managers are often outside the Scrum inner circle but are, nevertheless, important to the project. The team needs their support in getting the resources they need to meet commitments. But, as with other stakeholders, managers often have only a limited understanding of Scrum. They often do not realize that many of the techniques they use to manage their staff are in direct conflict with Scrum values and activities. Because of the power and authority managers hold, they can cause problems for the Scrum team in unique ways.

Agile Tip

"Done" has a special meaning in Scrum. When a requirement is done, it means it has the functionality agreed upon for that sprint between the Product Owner and team. It may require several sprints to create a feature the customer would call "done."

The Politician

The Problem

The Politician manager often vocally and enthusiastically supports trying an agile approach. He listens dutifully as teams explain how the Scrum process works. He hears that all requests for work must now go through the Product Owner. "No problem!" he says. "Great idea!" But like a shifty candidate for office, the Politician says one thing and does another. He says he supports Scrum, but in reality, his behavior doesn't change at all. He still interrupts the team, pulling members off to work on special projects "just this one time." He still makes schedule and feature commitments on the team's behalf and tells them to make it work. And he doesn't trust the Product Owner to oversee the product quality, so he steps into that role as well. And all the while he is doing this, he is singing the praises of Scrum and telling anyone who will listen how much he supports it.

Why This Happens

The Politician often has a trivial understanding of what it means not just to do Scrum but also to become an agile organization. In his mind, all the changes required from the enterprise to do Scrum well come from other people, not from him. He has not realized that, when an organization becomes agile, everyone must change. The Politician may, deep in his heart, think that Scrum is just a fad. He agrees to it to make the software development teams happy but never really internalizes the value of the framework. So when the rules of the framework clash with his own desires and management style, it is not hard to see which approach will win.

The Fix

When explaining Scrum to management for the first time, it is important to help them understand the benefits at an organizational level, not just a team level. These individuals must understand how Scrum is going to help them do their jobs. Since managers often have specific goals for revenue and profit, you need to be able to help them understand how Scrum will assist in achieving them. This will help managers begin internalizing the value of Scrum and make it easier for them to change their own behavior. As long as Scrum remains "something my teams do" rather than "something we all do," personalities like the Politician will continue to emerge from managers.

It falls to the ScrumMaster to help managers understand reasons behind the rules of Scrum. A good ScrumMaster can do this through clever questions and observations. For example, if the Politician wants to take a team member for another project after sprint commitments have already been made, the ScrumMaster can say, "So we already have a full sprint's worth of work. If you are taking Joe for a different project, that means we won't deliver everything we committed to. So what features would you like the Product Owner to remove out of this sprint?" Having this conversation helps the Politician realize his actions come at a cost and that tradeoffs must be made.

The ScrumMaster can also use the Politician's frequent speeches praising Scrum as an inroad to discussing the removal of impediments. When the Politician begins extolling the virtues of Scrum, the ScrumMaster can say, "I am so glad you feel that way because we need some help with a roadblock." Gradually, the ScrumMaster can help the Politician stand behind his words and understand his role in supporting the Scrum process.

The Slave Driver

The Problem

The Slave Driver is the consummate command-and-control manager. She believes the way to get the most from her staff is through tight control and oversight. The parts of the Scrum process that are most appealing to her are the areas of responsibility. She likes that teams must make commitments. She likes that the Product Owner will be held accountable for the overall success of the product. The part of Scrum she is not so thrilled with is the self-management. Deeply distrustful of this concept, the Slave Driver holds the fundamental belief that people will slack off if given the slightest chance. And, even if they don't slack off, they will still make poor decisions. In her mind, the only way to prevent these problems is through constant oversight and direction. The Slave Driver will often try to make commitments for the team, tell them how to meet those commitments, and let them know what kind of incremental progress on those commitments is acceptable. In short, the Slave Driver crushes self-management. Her teams either will be very frustrated or will simply give up trying to self-manage, allowing the boss to make every decision, no matter how big or small.

Why This Happens

The Slave Driver believes that, without her close direction, the team will make poor decisions. And, ironically, she is probably right. Slave Driver managers never give their teams a chance to strengthen their decision-making muscles. They get no practice weighing the pros and cons of a choice because the choice is constantly being made for them. Slave Driver managers often produce Sheep teams. Through their lack of confidence in the team and over-involvement in decision making, they crush a team's initiative and reduce them to a child-like state.

Slave Driver behaviors may also arise in those recently promoted to management from a technical position. In this case, they are still making the transition from "doing" to "managing." Often having more technical experience than those on the teams, they, understandably, tend to step in and give the "right answer" when the teams are struggling to solve a technical problem. In this case, the Slave Driver manager has not yet learned that part of being a good manager is teaching teams the decision-making process itself, not just handing out answers. The Slave Driver has yet to internalize the wise words of the *Tao Te Ching*:

> When the master governs, the people are hardly aware that she exists … When her work is done, the people say, "Amazing: we did it, all by ourselves!"

The Fix

This is another situation that can benefit from the ScrumMaster and Product Owner presenting a united front. Often, a Slave Driver is not aware of the subconscious reasons behind her behavior. In her mind, wanting to prevent the team from making mistakes is a perfectly good reason to step in and make decisions for them. Get to know the Slave Driver well enough that you can identify what metaphors might help her understand how damaging this

> **Agile Tip**
>
> In an agile organization, the role of management shifts from oversight and direction to that of removing impediments.

behavior is. For example, many people can understand the idea of self-management a bit better through the analogy of children. I will sometimes tell a Slave Driver manager, "Do you remember what it was like when your children first learned to walk? You needed to hold their hand and help with every step. Now that your children are teen-agers, do you still need—or want—to do that? No, you don't—because your goal was to teach them to walk on their own. Likewise, your goal as a leader should be to teach your teams to make decisions on their own." Analogies like this can be helpful because they will help the Slave Driver realize that what you are proposing is not so radical after all. Remind this manager, "You can't be here with the team every moment. Don't you want to have the confidence they will make good choices regardless? How will they learn to make those choices if they don't get practice?" Guidance like this will help a Slave Driver realize how unhelpful her interference is and how changing her behavior could ultimately benefit everyone.

The Brainstormer

The Problem

The Brainstormer gets good ideas by the minute and loves to share them with the team, the Product Owner, the ScrumMaster, people in the seat next to him on an airplane—pretty much anyone who will listen. Often a high-level manager—even a CEO, the Brainstormer is caught up in and enthralled by the latest and greatest. He comes to the Product Owner and team with new project ideas constantly, wanting to know how long it will take to "get this going." The team dutifully begins analyzing the business opportunity, but then—bam!—the Brainstormer has read an article or seen a television program with another good idea, and he wants to chase that. For the Scrum team and Product Owner, this can feel very much like being on the end of a leash with a hyper-active golden retriever. While essentially good-natured, the Brainstormer is an exhausting leader. In his excitement to experience and chase down all that is new in the world, this manager leaves his Product Owner and Scrum team struggling to keep up. They wonder if they should take anything he says seriously, knowing tomorrow it could all be forgotten in the wake of the next new and exciting idea.

Why This Happens

Ironically, the Brainstormer is doing exactly what those in upper management should do: developing strategy. It is good and right that senior managers should focus on what might grow the business in the future. Where the Brainstormer runs into trouble is in how he conveys those ideas. The work of a single Scrum team is essentially tactical, not strategic. They are concerned with meeting commitments for a sprint, not guiding the overall strategy of the company. So when the team hears, "We should get a mobile version of our latest app going," they interpret this as, "We should get a mobile version of our latest app going as soon as possible, ideally in the next sprint." In reality, this may not be what the Brainstormer meant. Often, this manager is really expressing the desire to discuss the idea, not implement it. Often highly verbal people, Brainstormers generate ideas best when they can talk through them with other people. But the team, used to getting fairly specific direction from the Product Owner ("I'd like to get these five features in the next sprint if possible") hears these requests not as invitations to discuss ideas but as directives to produce something.

Brainstormers may also not have an appreciation for how much time it takes to look into a new opportunity. If they are non-technical people, they often do not understand that even doing a cursory evaluation of a potential project or new technology can be a time-consuming effort. Coupling this lack of understanding of the effort involved to explore new opportunities with the inability to focus on any single idea for any reasonable length of time explains why Scrum teams run the other way when they see the Brainstormer coming.

The Fix

There are a couple of things that can improve interaction with a Brainstormer manager. First, help him understand that looking into new opportunities takes time. So this kind of work should be identified and prioritized on the product backlog, not squeezed into someone's spare time because, as we all know, spare time rarely materializes. Nothing happens "auto-magically." If the new opportunity is important enough to be placed on the product backlog, that helps the team understand that it really is something of value to the organization.

It may be hard for the Brainstormer to decide which ideas are worthy of being placed high on the product backlog without some input from the team. For this reason, it can be helpful to periodically invite this kind of manager to a product-backlog grooming session. Make it clear to the team that the purpose of this session is to discuss viability of new ideas, not how to implement them. Doing this will set the team at ease and help them hear new ideas without immediately feeling they have to determine how they can fit those ideas into a schedule. The Brainstormer gets what he needs—the chance to collaborate verbally—and the team also gets the benefit of being able to voice concerns and ideas.

It is worth noting that there is one individual in an agile organization who is unique in living in both the tactical and strategic world: the Product Owner. A good Product Owner has one eye on the day-to-day workings of the given sprint and another on the big picture, where the project needs to be not just at the end of the week but also, maybe, at the end of the year. He considers not just the needs of the sixty-person accounting team for whom you are building financial software but also the other people in the organization who might be affected by the changes. For this reason, the best defense against an overexcited Brainstormer is a good Product Owner. He can act as a filter between the team and the manager, listening to all ideas and requests and then working with the Brainstormer to decide which ones offer the highest potential benefit to the organization. One of the greatest gifts a Product Owner gives his team is practicing "expectation management" with stakeholders. Working with stakeholders to identify priorities allows the Product Owner to come to the team with a product backlog that is coherent, makes sense, and moves the organization in the direction it needs to go.

Combining Scrum Roles

One more major area where things can go amiss with roles is when they are combined. While it is not inherently wrong to combine some roles, there is always a cost to this action. One role, sooner or later, must be compromised to serve the other. Problems arise when a plan to deal with these compromises has not been made ahead of time. And when the roles combined are those both inside and outside the Scrum inner circle—such as a ScrumMaster who is also the team's manager—it gets even trickier. Scrum teams are unsure which hat this person is wearing when they make suggestions and become wary and untrusting. Finally, some roles simply cannot be combined in an agile organization. The very nature of the differing responsibilities makes these roles unsuitable for combining under any circumstance. Some common role combinations are listed below.

Big Brother

The Problem

Putting a person who already has inherent authority, such as a manager, into a role that is without authority, such as a ScrumMaster, can be a recipe for disaster. A ScrumMaster must facilitate and guide a team to self-management. A manager's job is oversight—in some ways, the very opposite of self-management. Conflicts can arise when the individual struggling to fill both these roles receives conflicting messages. On the one hand, she is told to remain non-directive with her Scrum team and let them self-manage. But she is also being told by her own management to obtain certain performance goals from her direct reports. When this happens, she is between a rock and a hard place with no good way to fulfill either role without compromising the other. Worse still, the team will sense her conflicting messages and lose trust in her. Wary of being judged poorly in their next performance review, they become unwilling to raise impediments and talk freely in front of her. She is no longer seen as their ScrumMaster but as a boss and representative of management. She has become Big Brother.

Why This Happens

It is not surprising that this role combination often fails. There are simply too many variables at play that can go wrong. First, the manager who serves as ScrumMaster must control her own behavior. She must have the ability to change hats when with the Scrum team and set aside her management authority. She must learn to give the team ideas and suggestions in a non-directive way. But even if she does that successfully, even if she comes into the Scrum meetings and says, "Listen, team, when we are in here, I am not your manager. I am your ScrumMaster," the team still has to believe her. In their minds, they may be thinking, "Yeah right. All I know is you write my annual performance review so I am not going to say anything in these meetings that makes me look as if I need help or don't know what I am doing." And even if the team and ScrumMaster are able to make these behavior changes successfully, the rest of the organization must also support this new approach. The Product Owner cannot tell the ScrumMaster-manager to make the team commit to a certain amount of work. He would, in effect, be asking her to don her management hat while in a ScrumMaster role, a clear conflict of interest.

The Fix

When this role combination works well, it is usually because it fits both the corporate culture and the individuals involved. Some teams say they like having their manager as a ScrumMaster. They say they have confidence she will protect them and look out for their best interests because that is what she does in her role as manager. Managers who fill the ScrumMaster role well often had a collaborative working style long before they encountered Scrum. It is in their nature to solicit ideas and encourage self-management. So transitioning to a ScrumMaster is an easy change for them. It is not unusual, in a single organization, to have some situations where the ScrumMaster-manager role combination works out fine and others where it does not. The key is keeping your eyes open to when it is not working. When a manager keeps her directive behavior or a team seems unwilling to take responsibility with her acting as their ScrumMaster, it is time to look at putting someone else into that role.

Superman

The Problem

The rhythm and pace of a Scrum project is more intense than that of typical project work. Everyone on this team rallies to deliver on the commitments the group has made. Because of this, the general tension and focus of a team tends to intensify as the sprint progresses, often peaking in the last day or two. For this reason, you should think long and hard before you put a single team member on more than one Scrum team. Conflicts are bound to happen. A Scrum team member plays a vital role in the requirements being delivered by Team A … but he also plays a vital role in the requirements being delivered by Team B. Which is more important? Even taking the time to think about and answer that question jeopardizes the health of both sprints and increases the likelihood that commitments will be missed and promises will be broken. The team member is left to figure out how to pull off this super-human feat—he is asked to be Superman.

Why This Happens

This problem frequently happens with team members who are specialists. This means they have a skill absolutely required by both projects but not needed (or allowed to be spared) full time. Database architects are an example of specialists. In such cases, it is possible and even desirable to have these individuals serve on more than one Scrum team, but some up-front planning is required.

There is also a desire to have the organization's best, most experienced technical people on every project. This can result in a senior technical person, often a technical lead, being assigned to several Scrum teams. While it is understandable to want senior people involved in key technical decisions, keep in mind that Scrum encourages team decision-making. It does so to avoid the very problem of being so dependent on a single person. If other team members must constantly defer decision-making to a senior technical person with no effort to cross-train or transfer knowledge, the organization is on its way to building a class system (see the Scrum team section on page 40).

The Fix

Individuals with specialized skills can rotate between Scrum teams as long as they have a clear schedule planned beforehand of when they are available for each given team. If they must serve two Scrum teams at once, then it should be clarified before conflicts arise how much time the specialist should give each team. A good rule of thumb is that every Scrum team member should be able to answer this question at any moment of the day, every day: "What is the most important thing I should be doing right now?" If the answer to that question is unclear due to conflicting priorities between projects, these problems must be resolved, or they will continue to surface repeatedly.

Likewise, senior technical people should move into a mentoring role. Even if the team looks to them for guidance, they should begin weaning them off that behavior as soon as possible. Of course, if a team member is working in an area that is completely new to him, he will need some guidance. But the ultimate goal is independence. In this way, a technical lead can eventually become less a Scrum team member and more an advisor. The team members can come to him with questions and for guidance when unsure but, otherwise, are able to operate independently.

Regardless of why you choose to put an individual on more than one Scrum team, there is one thing you must do for this arrangement to be successful. You must ensure the two teams have a staggered schedule, meaning their sprints cannot end on the same day. As we said earlier, the end of a sprint is an intense time for a Scrum team. Teams often take a "do whatever it takes" attitude to finish the sprint successfully. No matter how technically competent, if a single team member is asked to fully commit to two independent goals, he is set up to fail. People cannot be in two places at once. For this reason, Scrum teams that share some members should have sprints that end several days apart, ideally about a week.

Master of the Universe

The Problem

As we have seen, combining roles is fraught with risk. But there are some roles that should never be combined. To do so means you are no longer doing Scrum. Such is the case with combining the ScrumMaster and Product Owner roles. To understand why this is true, we must think back to one of the key goals of Scrum. The division of labor and responsibility in Scrum is designed to provide checks and balances of power. The three Scrum roles keep each other honest. They balance each other out for the overall benefit of the project. This is particularly true of the ScrumMaster and Product Owner. It is natural for a Product Owner to push a team. He is obligated to try to deliver as much value for the organization as possible. In the course of fulfilling this role, it is not unusual for a Product Owner to get a bit overzealous in his enthusiasm. That's when the ScrumMaster must step in. It is her obligation to protect the team and prevent them from being pressured into making commitments that they are in danger of missing. When the ScrumMaster and Product Owner roles are combined, this obligation becomes hopelessly blurred. A ScrumMaster facilitates and protects a team, but a Product Owner drives a team. When they are combined, you no longer have a Scrum role, you have a traditional project manager—all powerful and in charge. You have a Master of the Universe.

Why This Happens

There are two common situations in which organizations try to combine the ScrumMaster and Product Owner roles. The first is in very small companies. If your whole enterprise only has ten employees, it can be a little daunting to dedicate two people's time to filling Scrum roles. In a small company, some role combination is inevitable. But there are better solutions for small organizations than sacrificing the effectiveness of the Scrum framework. Likewise, another situation that produces the ScrumMaster-Product Owner combination is when the organization is just getting started with Scrum. In such situations, there is often one person who knows a great deal about Scrum. But no one else in the organization has any expertise yet. In this situation, it can be tempting for a ScrumMaster to also fulfill the Product Owner's role until someone can be trained. But doing so should be avoided. It is better to work with inexperienced people in the roles than to lump them together and call it "Scrum."

The Fix

Small organizations will, no doubt, have to combine roles. But a better choice for them is to have one person serve as both a Scrum team member and ScrumMaster. There will still be conflicts between roles, but they can be managed. Taking this approach acknowledges the fact that, in small companies, people wear many different hats. Yet the ScrumMaster and Product Owner roles, with their important balance of responsibilities, can remain separate.

For organizations that are just getting started with Scrum, the roles must also be split. The Scrum expert—the person with the most Scrum expertise—should take the role he feels most knowledgeable about and prepared to fill. But he should also plan to coach whoever will fill the other key role. As we said before, Scrum-Masters working with Product Owners who have not attended Scrum training should plan on spending nearly half their time coaching Product Owners and helping them get started. Needless to say, getting your Product Owner to

Agile Tip

Scrum chose to break apart the role of the traditional project manager into the ScrumMaster and Product Owner roles. This separation of duties benefits the teams, helping them work more effectively, and ultimately benefits the organization.

training should be a priority and can eliminate the temptation to combine the ScrumMaster and Product Owner roles.

As we have seen, some of the most common problems in an agile transformation come from difficulties in understanding how to effectively fill the Scrum roles. It is important to remember that everyone involved in your early Scrum projects has a set of behaviors and habits that are ingrained. Changing these habits, even when the desire to change is strong, can take time. Organizations new to Scrum should use the balancing power of the Scrum inner circle to keep participants honest. Doing Scrum well almost certainly requires major changes throughout the enterprise. Watch for the common problems with roles and nip them in the bud before they become ingrained. Doing so will ensure your organization can move onto the path of agile transformation and start reaping all the benefits it has to offer.

Week 2 – The Product Backlog

In Week 2 we'll focus on how to creating clear, actionable user stories. We'll learn how to build an effective product backlog as well as how to organize and maintain it over the life of the product.

Does this sound familiar?

1. Our user stories are either too big or too vague.

2. We don't understand what our Product Owner needs to call a user story "done."

3. Our user stories focus more on technical implementation details (the "how") than on business goals (the "what").

4. Priorities in our backlog constantly change, mostly based on who is yelling the loudest.

5. Our product backlog never has more than a sprint's worth of user stories, which makes it difficult for the team to do longer term technical planning.

6. Our Product Owner has multiple backlogs (one for new features, one for bugs, one for maintenance, etc.) so the team is never sure which one they should work on.

7. The team spends a lot of time working on tasks that have nothing to do with the sprint commitment or the user stories they have committed to deliver.

8. Our Product Owner never seems willing to call any user story "done."

9. Our product backlog has hundreds of items. It is too big to organize or understand.

10. Our Product Owner won't put his requirements in the form of a product backlog but instead gives the team a requirements specification, telling them "It's all in there. You guys figure it out."

Another common area where organizations experience problems implementing Scrum is in building and maintaining the product backlog. The kinds of problems you may experience will depend on your starting point. Organizations that create lots of heavy documentation often find they feel completely adrift when they move to a more agile approach. "We don't know what to build if you don't give us a design specification" is a common refrain from teams that are used to being spoon-fed requirements. On the other hand, smaller organizations that have worked in a very reactive way, setting priorities on a moment-by-moment basis, will likely feel the exact opposite. "Scrum is so restrictive," they will complain. "We have to make commitments for a whole two-week sprint. What if something comes up before that?" In reality, both kinds of organizations are just illustrating habits of ineffectiveness, each from opposite ends of the planning spectrum. Doing Scrum well requires understanding what constitutes "just enough" detail in a product backlog item. That level of detail varies, depending on the nature of the requirement itself, as well as where it lives (near the top versus near the bottom) on the product backlog. Let's look at the common problems enterprises experience when they are learning to build and maintain their product backlog.

Creating Backlog Items

As we learned earlier, a product backlog is a collection of physical and intellectual property and services a Product Owner is asking for. It could be software, user documentation, or even training. Each element of this collection is called a "product backlog item," or PBI for short. One very common form of PBI is a user story. A user story is not the same thing as a use case, which is a description of interactions between a user and a system. For our purposes, the definition of a user story is as follows:

- A business goal stated in a way that is independent of implementation

Let's look at two important parts of this definition. First, note the phrase, "independent of implementation." User stories focus on what we want to happen, not how we will make it happen. A key benefit to this is that a non-technical person, such as a stakeholder, can describe the business process she is trying to improve without having the technical background to understand how that function will be brought to life. Also note that a user story describes a business goal—an action a user of the system is actually trying to perform. Remember that a Product Owner must direct the overall vision of the product or project for which he has responsibility. The product backlog must be written in terms of business objectives so the Product Owner can weigh the benefits of the PBIs against one another to rank their priority. There are many different ways to write user stories. One approach is a simple statement of what should happen:

- A customer service representative can log notes from a customer call.

- A manager can view client billing totals by month.

- A serviceperson can mark a service order "complete."

Here is a popular template for user stories, which can be very useful.

- As a <type of user> I want to <take an action> so I can <achieve a result>.

This template for user stories can be particularly helpful in giving the Scrum team clues about the overall goal the Product Owner is trying to achieve with the user story and can call out subtle but important differences in details. For example, consider this user story:

- A user can register on the website.

It seems straightforward enough, doesn't it? But this statement really tells us nothing about why a user would want to register. Let's expand this user story using the template and look at three very different possibilities:

> **Agile Tip**
>
> In this book, the terms "requirement," "user story," and "product backlog item" (sometimes shortened to PBI) are used interchangeably. They are all descriptions of a deliverable listed on the product backlog.

1. As a website user, I want to register so the system will remember my personal information.

2. As a website user, I want to register so I can make a purchase.

3. As a website user, I want to register so I can use the system.

From user story number one, I would infer that visitors would want to register to gain the convenience of not having to enter their personal information every time they visit this website. In user story number two, it seems a user cannot make a purchase from the site without registering. And in user story number three, it appears a user cannot enter the site at all without first registering. In our example, each of these three user stories produces a registration process, but the goal of that process varies dramatically among the user stories. It is sometimes said that a good user story is a "promise for a future conversation." This means that user stories are the bud of a requirement—a starting point—but the conversations between the Scrum team, Product Owner, and stakeholders bring the true goal of the user story to light.

Given the importance of the product backlog in maximizing value to the business through good prioritization, it is not surprising that this is an area where problems crop up. The ability to write good PBIs is a learned skill. And even if the items are well written, they still need additional detail to understand when they would be considered done—this is acceptance criteria—and they have to be grouped in the backlog in a way that makes sense and is meaningful to both the Scrum team and the business itself. Let's look at some of the common areas where problems with the product backlog seem to appear.

User Story Composition

A good user story is:

- Small to moderate in size, meaning a body of work that can be completed in a few days (not weeks) of time
- Describes the business goal the user is trying to achieve
- Gives clues as to why this goal is valuable

Not surprisingly, one of the primary areas where those new to Scrum struggle is in creating user stories that fulfill these criteria. Here are some common problems with composing user stories.

The Kitchen Sink

The Problem

A Kitchen Sink user story is either too big or too vague. In truth, these user stories are often mini-projects in disguise. Sometimes also called "epics," the Kitchen Sink user story often does not describe a feature of the system so much as a whole area of functionality. Kitchen Sink user stories are often discovered in a product backlog grooming session. As the team begins asking questions of the Product Owner as to what level of functionality would be required to call the user story done, it becomes clear that the Kitchen Sink PBI is actually an amalgam of several user stories.

> ## Agile Tip
>
> An epic is a user story that is too big to be delivered in a single sprint. An epic must be broken down into a group of smaller stories before it can be considered for inclusion in a sprint commitment.

WEEK 2

Why This Happens

Kitchen Sink user stories are not bad so much as simply unrefined. It is natural, for example, when a project is just getting started, that many of the user stories will be Kitchen Sinks. When the functionality of the entire system is still being decided and the Product Owner is still thinking of features in the most vague terms, a few Kitchen Sink user stories are inevitable. It is also common for non-technical novice Product Owners to inadvertently write Kitchen Sink user stories. These individuals do not have the experience creating user stories to understand what constitutes "big." They need feedback from the Scrum team to understand when a user story is too big.

Kitchen Sinks cause trouble when they are near the top of the product backlog. It is not unusual for these PBIs to constitute several sprints' worth of work. Until they are broken down, the Scrum team will not be able to estimate them, nor will they feel comfortable committing to such a large body of work. Until a Kitchen Sink is parsed into its actionable and reasonably sized user story components, it is not ready to be implemented.

The Fix

One of the primary reasons for regular product backlog grooming sessions is to break down large user stories like Kitchen Sinks. During these meetings, the Product Owner and team can brainstorm what might go into fulfilling a PBI. This exercise will often give good clues as to what some of the individual user stories might be. To use a non-technical example, let's say I have the following user story:

- As a runner, I want to successfully complete the Boston Marathon so I can brag to my friends and family about it.

> ## Agile Tip
>
> Story-time meetings, also known as "product-backlog grooming sessions" or "backlog refinement meetings," are a great place to break down epics. They may also be used for creating user stories, estimating, and other activities that improve the quality of the product backlog.

Even if you are not a personal trainer, you can probably guess that there is a lot of work that precedes running the Boston Marathon. There is training, which might be further broken down into different types of training (speed work, hill work, long runs), running a qualifying race, registering, traveling to Boston, and no doubt many more elements. Then, too, what does it mean to me to "complete" this race? Does that mean if I am still standing at the end that is good enough? Or do I have some time goal I am aiming for? These are the types of questions the Product Owner and team will discuss in the Story-Time meeting, and from the answers, the smaller user stories that make up the Kitchen Sink will emerge.

It is important to note that it is much better to break down Kitchen Sinks in a Story-Time meeting than to wait to do so in the sprint-planning meeting. Remember the fundamental difference of goals for these two meetings: the ultimate goal of a Story-Time meeting is to improve the product backlog, but the ultimate goal of a sprint-planning meeting is to make a sprint commitment. A Scrum team will rightfully be frustrated with a Product Owner who uses his planning time to break down large user stories when they themselves need that time to consider their commitments.

It can be particularly useful to have a project management tool that allows Product Owners to break apart Kitchen Sink user stories but still keep them related under the umbrella of the original larger user story. Having this level of tracking helps the Product Owner track not only when the individual user stories are complete but also when the larger goal has been met as well.

The Instruction Manual

The Problem

Whereas a Kitchen Sink user story is too large or vague, an Instruction Manual user story has the opposite problem. It describes in painstaking detail not only what should be accomplished but also how. A typical Instruction Manual user story might look like this:

- As a marketing manager, I want to drag and drop a customer from one marketing group database to another.

The terms used here—"drag and drop" and "database"—are your first clue that this is not a well-written user story. It ventures too far into how the user story should be fulfilled but, at the same time, leaves out important information about why this PBI is valuable. A good Scrum team will push back on a Product Owner that presents such a PBI. They will say the user story does not describe the business goal so much as the path to get there. And they are right.

Why This Happens

Instruction Manual user stories sometimes originate from Product Owners who have technical backgrounds. Because they have inside knowledge about the workings of the system, they can tend to write user stories in the form of technical specifications. In their minds, as they are envisioning the user story, they are already also picturing how to fulfill it. This thought process comes through as they articulate the requirement.

Another way Instruction Manual PBIs crop up is when a non-technical Product Owner begins to adopt the language—the terms and phrases—he hears the team use. This is very natural thing to happen—the Product Owner hears the team throw out terms like "drag and drop" and "database change," and he starts using the terms as well. The dilemma of course is that, without technical knowledge, it is very easy to misuse these phrases and make the goals of the user story seem much more restrictive than they really are.

Product Owners must remember that the most useful thing they can do is write users stories that convey the business goal they are trying to achieve and why that goal is important. Then they can leave it to the team to suggest how that goal might be fulfilled.

The Fix

Scrum teams that are being asked to consider an Instruction Manual user story should try to get to the root of what the Product Owner is truly trying to achieve. A good way to start the conversation that will uncover that information is as follows:

- "I am not sure I understand exactly the goal of this user story. Help me understand—how do you do this today?"

In describing the current process, the Product Owner will often give good clues as to the business goal he is try to meet and how. For example, he might answer the above question like this:

- "Right now, I have a group of customers who receive our catalog for patio and deck furniture. Our research shows many of these customers also own boats so we would like to be able to cross-market boating accessories to this group as well. Right now, to get a customer into both groups, I have to put in a help desk ticket and wait at least a day or two. I want a quick, easy way to do this myself so I can eliminate that long delay."

You can see how one simple question—"How do you do this today?"—can yield a wealth of information. In this short paragraph we learned:

- The business goal we are trying to meet
- That customers will exist in both marketing groups—patio furniture and boat accessories—as opposed to mutually exclusive groups
- The pain-points of the current process, that it takes too long and makes the marketing manager feel as if he has no control over when the change will actually happen

With this information, we can now offer the Product Owner a better way to write this user story:

- As a marketing manager, I want to copy a customer from one marketing group to another so I can cross-market our patio and boat product lines.

Then the team can work with the Product Owner to define acceptance criteria that ensures the pain-points of the current process are improved.

Product Owners who have technical backgrounds will find their additional knowledge level to be a double-edged sword. On one hand, it can be nice to understand the technical implications of user stories. These factors do affect prioritization. On the other hand, with that level of knowledge, it is dangerously easy to become so focused on how the PBI will be fulfilled that the understanding of why it needs to be fulfilled in the first place gets lost. Scrum believes that the collective intelligence of the team will produce a solution that is ultimately better than anything any one person can come up with. Technical Product Owners must hold their desire to solve the problem in check. They must focus their efforts on making the end goal clear and then free the team up to come up with the best solution possible.

The Marching Orders

The Problem

Another issue can arise when PBIs are written to describe technical details rather than a business goal. In ordering the product backlog, a Product Owner with these kinds of user stories can be thinking in terms of when the work will be done rather than which user stories would yield the most business value. With this frame of mind, he orders the backlog like a technical specification. This is typical in an organization that has recently moved to Scrum from a more traditional project management approach. Used to writing out the work according to phases, at their worst, these PBIs look like this:

- Gather requirements for the customer details screen
- Add fields to the database
- Build the UI
- Connect UI and database

A backlog written in such a fashion gives a Product Owner almost no flexibility to move items around to yield more value. It also describes to the team not just how to fulfill given user stories (as with our Instruction Manual PBIs) but also how they should structure their entire body of work. They have been given Marching Orders.

Why This Happens

Ironically, Marching Orders can sometimes originate from the Scrum team itself. A particularly weak Product Owner, unsure of how to write good user stories, may turn to the team for advice. And the team, much more experienced at creating tasks rather than user stories, creates PBIs that reflect that experience. They look very task-like and are, in fact, most likely better suited as tasks. Unfortunately, creating a product backlog filled with tasks vastly reduces one of the key benefits of Scrum—the ability to move PBIs to gain more value. One mark of a good user story is that it is independent. This means it can stand on its own and, if fulfilled, give value to the business. Adding fields to a database, for example, is of no value to the Product Owner until those fields are available for use, usually through a user interface. While it is true that user stories with a given project all have some relation to one another (they are, after all, part of the same project), Product Owners should aim to keep them loosely rather than tightly coupled. Marching Order user stories reduce flexibility and limit everyone's ability—the Scrum team's and the Product Owner's—to use the benefits of Scrum to improve the overall quality of the end deliverable.

The Fix

Marching Order user stories are a sign that the Product Owner does not understand how to write good PBIs. So some remedial education is in order. If the entire organization is unsure what constitutes a good user story or how to tell the difference between a user story and a task, consider getting a good Scrum coach to come onsite and provide some training. If there are members of other teams (ScrumMasters, Scrum team members, or Product Owners) that already know how to create good user stories, they may be able to help educate other teams. But whether you use internal or external resources, don't put off correcting Marching Order user stories. Organizations that have product backlogs filled with Marching Order user stories get very frustrated with Scrum. They feel they are doing everything right, and yet, the process does not yield appreciably better results than a more predictive, waterfall approach. Only when user stories are written as independent entities describing business value can the true value of Scrum emerge.

Determining Priority

Once a few user stories have been written, it is time for the Product Owner to begin the process of prioritization. A good Product Owner will take several factors into consideration when prioritizing the backlog. Questions he may ask himself are:

- Which user stories would I like to see up and working first?

- Which user stories, if fulfilled, would help us gain support from the stakeholders?

- Which user stories are small and could give us quick wins?

- Which user stories, if fulfilled, would please our management the most?

- Which user stories give the most value to the product itself?

You will notice that there is a varied list of factors that go into the business value of a given user story. A good Product Owner does not rely solely on a canned return-on-investment calculation to prioritize his backlog. Certainly, those metrics have their place in determining the overall value of a given PBI. But a wise Product Owner is shrewd. He knows there are more factors at play than mere numbers in a spreadsheet. Keeping the project moving towards its overall goal of delivering value while considering all the not-so-obvious issues that affect priority is the "art" part of the art and science of being a Product Owner.

So, not surprisingly, Product Owners sometimes experience problems prioritizing their backlogs. They may focus on the wrong things when deciding order. Or they may have old behaviors from a previous role that creep into their decision-making processes. They may not have good decision-making "muscles." Regardless of how things go wrong, a poorly prioritized product backlog can put an entire project's value to the organization in jeopardy. It is important to spot these patterns early and correct them through guidance and education.

WEEK 2

The Screamer's List

The Problem

A Screamer's List is a product backlog that is ordered solely by one criterion: who is yelling and complaining most loudly at the moment. Far from trying to provide overall product direction and return on investment, the Product Owner creating this backlog is in survival mode. His goal is to avoid making people unhappy. Unfortunately, clever stakeholders quickly learn to exploit this weakness for their own gain. They learn they can put the pressure on, raise their voices, email requests for backlog items with every manager in the company cc'd—all with the express purpose of getting their way. Like spoiled children, they learn they can get their way by throwing a tantrum. And as the Product Owner gives in to this kind of behavior, he reinforces it, assuring it will happen again. Quite aside from its lack of business value consideration, prioritizing a backlog this way has an obvious drawback. Sooner or later, this unfortunate Product Owner is going to have *two* Screamers, each wanting his work completed in the next sprint. But there will be room for only one. For this Product Owner, his worst nightmare has come true. He is going to make someone, maybe multiple someones, very unhappy indeed.

Why This Happens

Product Owners who fall prey to creating a Screamer's List may feel they do not have the right to tell anyone no. However, this is exactly what they sometimes must do. In fact, if there is a single characteristic that can very effectively predict how well an individual will perform as a Product Owner, it is this: the willingness to make tough decisions, even if some of his stakeholders are unhappy with those decisions.

How can that be? Aren't Product Owners supposed to work with their stakeholders to gather and articulate requirements? Yes, they are. But that doesn't mean every one of those requirements will yield enough benefit to be added to the product. Product Owners live in a world of costs and benefits. They must always ensure the backlog reflects, to the best of their ability, the highest overall value to the organization. Determining this value means sometimes having to make tough choices. But when they create a Screamer's List, they are, in effect, looking to help themselves, not the organization.

Product Owners should get used to the idea early on that sometimes they will have to say "no" or, at the very least, "not yet."

The Fix

Product Owners will have an easier time saying no to creating a Screamer's List if they have the support of their management, their ScrumMaster, and the Scrum team. If these individuals and groups make it clear the Product Owner has final say on product backlog issues, the person in that role will feel empowered to make these decisions. The ScrumMaster can help this process during product-backlog grooming sessions. As stakeholders raise suggestions for features to be added to the system, she can point out that they are just that—suggestions. Features should be described as being "for consideration for inclusion in the product backlog" at this stage. Then, instead of yelling and threatening, the stakeholders can focus on explaining to the Product Owner why the feature would be valuable. This focus on defining business value is a much more productive mindset from which to make prioritization decisions.

It probably goes without saying that it is particularly damaging when the stakeholders who are screaming are the Product Owner's managers. When a manager publicly overrules a Product Owner, she sends the message that the Product Owner isn't really in charge of requirements. This can open the door to other stakeholders trying to work around the Product Owner to get what they want.

Managers and Product Owners should present a united front to the public. In private, they can hash out the relative merits of individual PBIs and argue with one another. But by the time the rest of the stakeholders see the ordered product backlog, these two must be in agreement. Organizations rarely have enough money and time to add infinite features to a given product. Part of the power of Scrum is that there is an individual, the Product Owner, charged with making careful decisions about the best way to spend limited resources. And the sooner the stakeholders come to respect that fact, the faster an organization will begin seeing the benefits.

WEEK 2

The Moving Target

The Problem

A product backlog is expected to change over the life of the project. More dramatic changes often occur near the beginning of a project, when many requirements are still being discovered along the way. But this tends to diminish as the project goes along. When that doesn't happen, when requirements seem to swing wildly from sprint to sprint with no pattern or improvement in predictability over the life of the project, the backlog becomes a Moving Target. Teams grow frustrated as they build a feature in one sprint only to undo that work and build it a different way in the next one. An issue or feature might be raised as an emergency this week, only to be completely forgotten next week. Moving Target backlogs have no cohesiveness. There is no overall plan. Because of this lack of thoughtful direction, projects with such backlogs are often very expensive, first wandering one direction and then veering off on another path with no comprehensive strategy or end goal in mind.

Why This Happens

Product Owners are responsible for overall product direction and managing return on investment. When a Product Owner creates a Moving Target backlog, he is fulfilling neither responsibility. This most often occurs when the Product Owner is not being held accountable by the rest of the organization. In the early stages of Scrum adoption, the Product Owner may still have his "real" job in addition to his new Scrum role. He may think of his responsibilities as those of his original job and anything to do with Scrum as work for his spare time. This kind of attitude often creates a Product Owner that does not give prioritization of the backlog the careful thought and consideration it needs. When such a laissez-faire attitude about product-backlog prioritization is coupled with no real responsibility for the decisions being made or money being spent, a Moving Target backlog is a natural outcome.

The Fix

Product Owners must be held accountable by the organization for fulfilling their role well. They must be able to justify the backlog prioritization, as well as money and time spent. Until they do this, they are not truly acting as a Product Owner. Of course, part of being a good Product Owner is having the

time to do the job well. As long as the organization sends the message that this role is something
to be fulfilled on the side, as an afterthought, it
will be very difficult for a Product Owner, even
one with good intentions, to succeed. Being a
Product Owner is a full-time job. Organizations
must recognize that when an individual steps
into this role, he has effectively stepped into a
new job, not an additional one. To avoid Moving
Target backlogs, the Product Owner must have
both the time and the accountability to be successful in the role.

> ## Agile Tip
>
> It is normal for the product backlog
> to change in each sprint as more
> business needs become known.
> But each change to the backlog
> must be accompanied by careful
> consideration by the Product Owner.

WEEK 2

The Disguised Waterfall

The Problem

One reason to engage the services of an agile coach is to avoid making begin-
ners' mistakes. Though agile, like many other things, can be learned via the
school of hard knocks, there is no reason to take such a painful approach. An
experienced agile coach can spot common mistakes early, especially those
an organization is making due to old patterns of doing work, and help teams
avoid going down non-productive paths.

One such problem pattern is exhibited by organizations that previously
used a phased approach for project management. The planners in such enterprises tend to think in terms of completing work in a linear fashion—determine requirements, design, build, test, and deploy—because that is what a
phased approach requires. Often the artifacts of one phase—a requirements
document, for example—must be signed off before the next phase can begin.

When such individuals become Product Owners, it may be difficult for
them to let go of this way of thinking. Hence, they will structure their backlog
not with user stories that provide whole pieces of useful functionality but,
instead, with activities from their old project management methodology.
The top priority PBIs will be "requirement user stories," followed by stories
for design, then ones for building, testing, and finally deployment. When
Product Owners organize their backlog in this fashion, they are not taking
an agile approach at all. Instead, they have created a product backlog that is
a Disguised Waterfall, just as they used to organize work before.

Why This Happens

Disguised Waterfall backlogs occur when there is a lack of understanding about what a product backlog item is. Recall that we said good PBIs are independent of one another. Another characteristic of a good PBI is that it is valuable, meaning valuable to the customer who will be using it. When a Product Owner is used to creating a more traditional project-management plan, he tends to think of a structure in terms of tasks and how to break down the work. However, these things are not the same as PBIs. A good PBI will yield value on its own rather than by simply being a step in the process of fulfilling a much larger PBI.

For example, suppose I am a Product Owner who owns a yoga studio. My team is building a website to share information about my business with customers. I may have a user story in my backlog that looks like this:

- "As a yoga studio owner, I want to have contact information on my website so my customers know how to get in touch with me."

This is a perfectly good PBI. It will yield value to the studio owner when it is fulfilled. In a Disguised Waterfall backlog, you might see the same user story broken out as follows:

- "As a yoga studio owner, I want to gather the requirements for the contact page."

- "As a yoga studio owner, I want to create the design document for the contact page."

- "As a yoga studio owner, I want to code the contact page."

And so on. But in reality, what the yoga studio owner really wants, what she will ultimately find useful, is the finished contact page. So that is what the user story should describe.

Disguised Waterfall PBIs sometimes occur when the Product Owner has difficulty breaking down a large user story into smaller stories. In our original example above, the team may say, "This user story sounds too big—you need to break it down." If a Product Owner is unsure how to break out the large Kitchen Sink user story he may fall back into old patterns of listing the tasks or steps as individual user stories. But in reality, these are not true user stories because the Product Owner will not truly have anything useful until all the PBIs that go into creating a contact page are fulfilled.

The Fix

Another characteristic of a good user is that it is negotiable. What that means in this context is that a user story should always be able to be made smaller by limiting functionality. But doing this takes some practice, particularly for those coming from traditional project management. Let's revisit our yoga studio owner and her contact page again. Suppose the reason the team said this story was too big was because she defined it as follows:

- Show address
- Show a map
- Have emails of all instructors listed
- Have instructor bios
- Describe our yoga philosophy
- Allow customers to submit questions
- Allow customers to register for classes

And more. This could very well be a Kitchen Sink user story, too big for the team to commit to in a given sprint. But rather than creating a Disguised Waterfall backlog of steps that lead to all this functionality, the Product Owner should break down the large user story into pieces that are useful on their own, as in this example:

- As a yoga studio owner, I want to show our address and phone number on the contacts page.

This useful PBI, regardless of whether the map, email, instructor bios, or anything else is included, would allow customers to find the yoga studio and contact them. More functionality could be added later like this:

- As a yoga studio owner, I want to have emails of instructors listed in our site.

In looking at these two PBIs, the Product Owner would probably say it is more valuable to display the address and phone number of the studio than

WEEK 2

the instructors' emails. So he would prioritize the first user story higher on the backlog than the second. But regardless of prioritization, both PBIs give something of value that actually works—something customers can use. Unlike a Disguised Waterfall backlog, PBIs written this way allow the Product Owner maximum flexibility to move items around the backlog to get more value.

Organizing the Product Backlog

We've said that the product backlog is a living artifact, changing in each sprint as PBIs are fulfilled, added, or removed because they are no longer desired. A novice Product Owner can often underestimate the amount time he needs to maintain the product backlog. Holding consistent backlog-grooming meetings with the Scrum team, ScrumMaster, and stakeholders will help with this. Having regularly scheduled meetings during each sprint to improve the product backlog will make sprint-planning meetings go much more smoothly.

If the Product Owner does not allow adequate time for product-backlog maintenance, or if the grooming sessions are ineffective, the result can be a disorganized product backlog. Even if the user stories themselves are well-written, if the backlog is not organized in a coherent manner, the project will suffer. Let's look at some common problems with product-backlog organization.

The Starvation Diet

The Problem

When a Product Owner does not allow adequate time to build and maintain the product backlog or he thinks only in tactical terms of what should be created in the next sprint, he is in danger of creating a Starvation Diet backlog. The most common symptom of such a backlog is that the Scrum team often runs out of work. They find themselves continually having to go back to the Product Owner before the end of the sprint to say, "OK, we're finished. Now what do you want us to do?" A Starvation Diet backlog may well leave a team sitting idle with no work to do.

Another issue with the Starvation Diet backlog is that it gives the team no sense of the overall direction of the project. For example, the Product Owner may have a user story high on the backlog about a customer being able to make a payment via credit card. There may be another PBI further down the backlog about that same customer being able to set up recurring credit card payments. Being able to see both user stories, even if they are positioned far apart in the backlog, will help the team understand how that feature may expand in functionality, and they can plan accordingly in their design. When a team never gets to see user stories that expand beyond one sprint, they can never plan or design for future desires.

> ## Agile Tip
> Good Scrum teams can produce an astonishing amount of work. When the organization is still adapting to this new pace, backlog starvation is a common problem.

Why This Happens

A Product Owner may create a Starvation Diet backlog because he is carrying the real contents of the backlog in his head. Thinking in a tactical, sprint-by-sprint manner, he may not understand how his revealing so little of the overall plan for the project is limiting the team's ability to support him. This is another behavior that can stem from old habits. If the Product Owner was previously in a role where he fed requirements to a team in piecemeal fashion—for example, as a technical lead—it can be easy to slip back into that pattern.

But certainly, the most common reason for a Starvation Diet backlog is the Product Owner not putting adequate time into product-backlog maintenance. As we've said before, being a Product Owner is a full-time job. Working with the stakeholders to identify and articulate requirements, with the team to define and put scope around requirements, making prioritization decisions—these activities are time consuming. A Product Owner that does not give the job adequate time is likely to leave his team looking for something to do.

The Fix

The first step in avoiding a Starvation Diet backlog is holding regular backlog-grooming sessions. This allows an overwhelmed Product Owner the chance to schedule time within the sprint—every sprint—to work on improving the Product Backlog. It can be helpful to use these meetings as brainstorming sessions with stakeholders to actually write new-product backlog items. Taking the time to teach stakeholders how to write good user stories will free up the Product Owner's time. Instead of feeling he has to write every single PBI himself, he can focus instead on prioritizing the backlog items. It is important to remember that anyone can create backlog items—which the Product Owner prioritizes. When others in the organization—stakeholders, the Scrum team, even the ScrumMaster—help with this manual labor, it can often eliminate the problem of a Starvation Diet backlog.

The Product Owner should also be realistic about how many stakeholders he can gather requirements from. If, for example, his project involves gathering requirements from five hundred customers at multiple sites, he should recognize this is probably more work than one person can reasonably be expected to manage on his own. For large projects, it is not unusual for a Product Owner to have his own team of helpers—business analysts, user interface designers, tech writers—that help gather and articulate requirements. Making sure the Product Owner has a reasonable work statement will improve his chances of coming to the next sprint-planning meeting well prepared and with a comprehensive product backlog.

The Laundry List

The Problem

It is not unusual, early in a project, to have a Starvation Diet backlog. But as a project goes on over perhaps many releases, the opposite problem can occur. Backlogs can get huge with truly useful features mixed in with fluff, wish-list features, and items that are no longer even needed or wanted. Even if the backlog is prioritized reasonably well, these Laundry List backlogs are cumbersome for the Product Owner and Scrum team alike. Truly valuable backlog items tend to get lost amid less valuable work. And it is hard for a team to look at a Laundry List backlog and get a sense of how the individual items might be grouped together to provide the most value in a given sprint. Facing a Laundry List backlog in a Story-Time meeting is harrowing for everyone involved. The idea of combing through a backlog of, say, fifteen hundred items can quickly put everyone into a coma. Backlog items start to all look alike, and it is hard to develop goals for improving such a backlog because the work statement is so daunting.

Why This Happens

Laundry Lists can occur when product backlogs become dumping grounds for requirements. A Product Owner must keep his backlog well groomed.

That includes not only adding new requirements as they arise but also regularly scanning the backlog for outdated requests. This issue can arise, like so many others, when the Product Owner underestimates the amount of time required to build and groom the product backlog. Even if the backlog is regularly refined, PBIs must have some basic information attached to them—for example, date of creation and who requested the feature—so a Product Owner can quickly determine if they describe functionality that is still needed.

The Fix

Certainly, regular grooming can help avoid the problem of a Laundry List backlog. But there is often a reluctance on the Product Owner's part to actually delete backlog items. It can be helpful, from both a historical and political aspect, to have a written record of who asked for what, when. Then, too, it is quite possible to have large backlogs filled with legitimate items. To keep a large backlog intact but make it more manageable, the Product Owner may choose to "granularize" or chunk it. When a backlog is granulized, it is divided into meaningful chunks that then can be discussed and planned for as a body of work. For example, it is common for commercial software companies to have a regular release schedule—perhaps quarterly. In that case, a large backlog could be broken down into more manageable pieces as follows:

Product Backlog		
September Release	**December Release**	**March Release**
PDI #1	PBI #1	PBI #1
PBI #2	PBI #2	PBI #2
PBI #3	PBI #3	PBI #3
PBI #4	PBI #4	PBI #4
PBI #n	PBI #n	PBI #n

WEEK 2

Using this technique gives more focus to a Laundry List backlog and makes discussion about future releases easier. If quarterly releases are not applicable to your situation and no other categorization scheme comes to mind, consider using front burner, back burner, and freezer. You have flexibility in how you define these categories, but one possibility is:

- Front burner—backlog items planned for the next couple sprints

- Back burner—backlog items planned for the near future but not in the next couple sprints

- Freezer—backlog items that are not currently scheduled to go into the product but still contain valuable information and may be completed in the future

Using this technique, the Product Owner can keep the backlog fresh and meaningful by periodically scanning the freezer and back burner to determine which items should be promoted to the front burner.

The Self-serve Buffet

The Problem

A Product Owner may go a step beyond chunking the product backlog and divide work into completely separate product backlogs. For example, he may have a "new features" backlog, an "enhancement" backlog, and a "bug" backlog. While at first this categorization into separate lists might seem a good idea, the dilemma comes when the team is unsure which backlog to work from. The whole purpose of a product backlog is to make completely clear the order in which the team should deliver items. With multiple backlogs in play, the answer to this question becomes muddled. There is a more insidious problem as well. Too often bug backlogs, in particular, are expected to be addressed in the Scrum team's spare time. A Product Owner is reluctant for them to allot actual sprint time to this work and instead hopes it will somehow "auto-magically" be done in those mythical hours per day when the team finds itself with nothing to do. A busy Scrum team may find these downtimes do not materialize. With direction as to what should be done first left unclear, the team itself must choose. They pick at the multiple backlogs like a self-serve buffet—a little of this, a little of that. When this happens, the Product Owner has effectively given prioritization of the backlog to the team.

Why This Happens

Multiple backlogs can be a Product Owner's attempt to make sense of a too-large list of requirements. Knowing he has a Laundry List on his hands, he naturally concludes he should divide the work into logical categories. And while this organization may help the Product Owner better see how much of each kind of work he has (for example, new features vs. bugs), it does nothing to help the Scrum team understand what work has the highest priority. Scrum teams are in the business of making and meeting commitments, not assigning business value and prioritizing.

> ## Agile Tip
>
> The Product Owner should regularly clean the backlog and remove outdated items that are no longer needed.

Providing them multiple backlogs inevitably leads to confusion and to the Product Owner not taking full responsibility for directing the development of the product itself.

The Fix

While it is fine for a Product Owner to divide backlog items into categories—new features, bugs, enhancements—for his own planning purposes, when it is time for sprint planning and commitments, the team must be presented with a single prioritized backlog containing all deliverables the Product Owner expects. And the Product Owner must be realistic about the fact that all work takes time. Instead of expecting the team to find spare hours to address bugs, the benefit of having those bugs fixed should be weighed against the benefit of delivering new functionality. In this way, the Product Owner can make overt choices about which PBIs yield more value. And most important, he maintains responsibility for determining priority, rather than effectively turning that duty over to the team.

As you can gather from this section, organizing and maintaining a product backlog takes a lot of effort. Product Owners would do well to devote regular time in their schedules for this work. Backlogs truly are living artifacts. They will grow and change over the life of the product. Spending the extra effort to keep the backlog well organized will pay dividends to both the Product Owner and team as they work together to bring the backlog items to life.

Adding Acceptance Criteria

Once PBIs are written and organized in the backlog, the next step is under-standing what is required to call a given PBI "done." Look at the following user story:

> "As an online shopper, I want the store to save my information so I don't have to re-enter it every time."

This is a perfectly good user story and explains clearly what the Product Owner is expecting from the perspective of a customer's experience. But it is unlikely a team would be willing to commit to such a user story without a bit more information. For example, what data is included in "my informa-tion"? Name? Address? Payment details such as credit card number? Should there be an option to save non-financial data only? These are some of the questions a team might ask a Product Owner when trying to determine the scope of a user story. The answers to these questions form the acceptance criteria of the PBI. They establish the boundaries of a user story. Without such details, it would be hard for the Product Owner and team to determine when a particular user story could be considered done.

Acceptance criteria are developed through conversations and negotia-tions between the Product Owner and team. Story-Time meetings and sprint planning are two logical times for this to occur. The screenshot below shows a user story with acceptance criteria added. The acceptance criteria are often preceded by the words "definition of done" or "done when" to indicate these are the criteria that must be met before the story can be considered done.

> ## Agile Tip
>
> Acceptance criteria represents the agreement between the Product Owner and team about what are required to call a specific user story "done."

Getting good acceptance criteria is a skill learned best through practice and experience. Unfortunately, that experience often comes through writing bad acceptance criteria and getting burned by the negative results. Below are some common problems with the techniques that teams and Product Owners use to define their acceptance criteria.

The Mind Reader

The Problem

When a team is first learning to work with the Product Owner to develop acceptance criteria, individual team members can be reluctant to ask for clarification when they need it. Sometimes this is because they don't want to appear stupid, as if they don't know something that must surely be obvious to everyone else. Or they may feel that asking for more details about a particular PBI might be seen as challenging the validity of the requirement. Whatever the root cause, team members who are unsure what a requirement means but are unwilling or unable to ask for clarification take the only other path possible to answer these questions: they make assumptions. Instead of asking for more information, the team member becomes a Mind Reader, choosing to use his psychic powers to decide what a Product Owner means when describing a PBI.

Why This Happens

Defining acceptance criteria is part science and part art. It requires good communication skills and, in particular, an awareness about not just what is being described in a requirement but also what is being implied. Not everyone has had the opportunity to develop these abilities. When a team member has a lack of communication skill, he can fall into the Mind Reader pattern because he does not yet know a better approach. Likewise, some Mind Readers lack confidence. They may find the Product Owner slightly intimidating. In these cases, asking the Product Owner for clarification feels too uncomfortable, so making assumptions seems to be the safer choice.

The Fix

The good news is that being an effective communicator is a learned skill and one that individuals can improve over time. The ScrumMaster and Product Owner can support the team as they learn to ask better questions to develop acceptance criteria. ScrumMaster should actively observe the conversations to develop acceptance criteria. They can help less confident team members save face by asking questions they think the team might be thinking. In this way, too, they model the appropriate behavior for the team to follow.

WEEK 2

Gradually, as the team learns and mimics these patterns of questions, the ScrumMaster can step out of the conversations.

The Product Owner can help this process, as well, by keeping a patient and positive attitude during acceptance criteria discussions. Product Owners are often people in management roles, and they can be quite intimidating to more junior team members. It takes only one experience of being carelessly snapped at ("That's completely obvious! What a dumb question!") to crush a team member's confidence and have him revert to the Mind Reader pattern. Instead, when the Product Owner receives the team's questions positively ("Good question" or "I'm glad you asked that") and follows up with the requested details, he is giving the team the confidence to ask more questions in the future.

Motherhood and Apple Pie

The Problem

Even if a team and Product Owner are able to hold effective discussions about the boundaries of a given user story, those discussions don't always yield good acceptance criteria. The mark of good acceptance criteria is that it materially affects the size of the PBI. For example, consider this user story:

- As an athlete, I want to compete in a marathon so I can become a long-distance runner.

If I were a personal trainer and received this user story from a client, a couple of my first questions for her would be:

- "When do you want to do the race?"
- "Are you currently running?"
- "Do you have a time goal you want to meet?"

Suppose she answered my questions in the following manner:

"I want to do the race fairly soon. I am running some—a few times a week. And as far as a time goal, I am hoping to be pretty fast."

The acceptance criteria she has given me here is too vague to be of use. Does "fairly soon" mean some time in the next few weeks or in the next couple years? Stating she is running "a few times a week" tells me nothing about her actual mileage or training frequency. And what is "pretty fast" to this client? Twelve-minute miles or seven-minute miles? Clearly, before we can determine the work statement of this particular user story, I need to get more specifics about the desired end state of this user story.

Teams and Product Owners will sometimes describe the boundaries of PBIs with such uncertain terms. They will have acceptance criteria with vague, implied meanings, such as "It should be fast" or "It should be easy to use." The problem is these amorphous descriptions do nothing to limit the scope of a user story. You would be hard pressed to find any system that users did not want to be fast and easy to use. They are ubiquitous desires for general goodness, like motherhood and apple pie. But what those terms mean in the context of a given system can vary greatly. For this reason, such vague terms are not good candidates for acceptance criteria.

Why This Happens

A Product Owner and team's first foray into discussions about user-story details can often yield Motherhood and Apple Pie acceptance criteria. But it is important not to stop there. More detail is needed. Teams must recognize that such vague statements as "It should be fast" are not acceptance criteria but rather a clue as to where the real acceptance criteria may lie—in more discussions about what, exactly, "fast" means.

Motherhood and Apple Pie acceptance criteria may also stem from the fact that the Product Owner has not thought through what these terms really mean to him. He himself may be unsure not only of what constitutes a "fast" system but also of what is even possible. He may include such vague acceptance criteria in hopes that the team will know more than he does and implement something that will please the end users and meet their needs.

The Fix

In all cases, the cure for Motherhood and Apple Pie acceptance criteria is more discussion. Statements like "It should be fast" should immediately spark a discussion as to what "fast" means in this particular context. If team members are not stepping in to ask these questions, the ScrumMaster again has a chance to model the appropriate behavior. Asking the Product Owner to clarify and paraphrasing the resulting answers—"So you are looking for a response in less than one second?"—will help team members learn valuable

WEEK 2

negotiation skills that they can use in these and many other discussions with the Product Owner.

Needle in a Haystack

The Problem

Many Product Owners choose to use documentation outside of their user stories to capture details about the requirements. There is absolutely nothing wrong with this. In fact, it can be a great way to provide the team with additional details. The problem comes when those details are in large requirements documents or specification and there is no clear indication from the Product Owner as to where in the document the details about a given user story are written. In such cases, nearly every user story will have a note in its acceptance criteria like this: "See BRD 'Project X.'" Since these documents can be quite large—sometimes more than one hundred pages for a large project, the team is forced to sift through pages searching. Like looking for a needle in a haystack, they spend an unnecessarily long time getting the details of each requirement as they go through all the pages, trying to find the one or two paragraphs that are applicable.

Why This Happens

Many people who move into the Product Owner role were formerly business or requirements analysts. These individuals often have a high level of comfort with traditional documentation like business requirements documents (BRDs) and less confidence in writing requirements in a user story format. Because of this disparity, they may unconsciously put less effort and time into their user stories, knowing that the "real requirements" are in the BRD. Then, too, if this Product Owner could, in the past, simply hand a team a BRD and expect them to work through it on their own, it may not occur to this individual that a more targeted approach would be better.

The Fix

There is an easy solution to the Needle in a Haystack problem. In each user story that references an outside document, the Product Owner can add the general location of the information. Adding "See BRD 'Project X' pages 45–46" is much more helpful than simply directing the team to the BRD as a whole. It is common to reference outside documentation in user stories. Trying to define every possible nuance of a user story through acceptance criteria is not only unnecessary but makes the user stories unwieldy and hard to manage. Acceptance criteria form the boundaries of the user story, helping the team understand what is and is not in scope for this particular requirement. But when it comes time to start building, more details can be helpful. Specific direction as to where to find those details is always appreciated by the team. Organizations with electronic tools for agile product management find they can put links directly in the user stories to electronic versions of the needed documents.

Adding Tasks

Once a user story and its acceptance criteria are well defined, the next step is usually for the team to begin to identify the tasks required to complete the work. Those new to Scrum sometimes get user stories and tasks confused, but in reality they are very different. Whereas user stories are about *what* needs to be created, tasks focus on *how* to bring the requirement to life. Understanding the tasks that go into fulfilling a particular user story can aid a team in many ways. Many teams prefer to identify the major tasks behind a requirement before they attempt to do estimation. They feel knowing more about the work itself will give them clues as to how much effort would be involved in delivering a given requirement. Identifying tasks also gets the team thinking about who will do which tasks and can alert them to bottlenecks. Finally, as tasks are completed each day and moved to a "done" status, the Product Owner gets a sense of progress on the overall sprint commitment.

Tasks may be extremely detailed or may be more high-level. Different teams have different preferences, and since tasks exist primarily for the team to help them manage their work, they should use task definition techniques that work best for them. However, many teams have problems with how they define and use tasks. When that happens, they should look at additional techniques that will help them approach tasking more effectively. Following are some common issues with tasks.

The Blob

The Problem

Some teams define their tasks at an extremely high level. In such cases, it is not unusual to see a large user story with only two defined tasks: 1) build it and 2) test it. There are several problems with such Blob tasks. First, there may actually be several sub-tasks involved in "test it," including writing test scripts, generating test data, building automated regression tests, and similar activities. When doing estimates, the team may forget about some of these when considering the size of a user story, thereby under-sizing it. There may also be implied tasks, such as setting up the test environment which are not explicitly mentioned but, nevertheless, take the team's time. Finally, it is hard for a Product Owner to understand the progress being made on a user story when a single task may sit in the "in progress" state for several days. In reality, work may be moving along just fine but, because no tasks move to a "done" state, there is no visible evidence as such.

Why This Happens

Teams that create Blob tasks may be used to carrying the work they need to do in their heads. It may be difficult for them, at first, to articulate all the steps involved in "test it" such that they can be written down. But a more common reason for Blob tasks is that the team has not actually thought through what tasks must be completed to fulfill a PBI. They create a generic "test it" task with the idea that they will work out the details later. The danger in this is that they are working out those details after a sprint commitment has been made. The key risk here is that there are time-consuming tasks which were not taken into consideration before making the commitment. When that happens, the team and Product Owner can be unpleasantly surprised as PBIs end up being much larger than first anticipated.

> **Agile Tip**
>
> A good rule of thumb is that a task should be a body of work that takes about a day or less to complete.

The Fix

Teams should focus on having appropriate task granularity. This means most tasks should take a day or less to complete. Keeping tasks at this level will ensure that there are almost always tasks being moved to the "done" state on a daily basis. This gives the Product Owner a better sense of progress and gives the ScrumMaster a warning sign of potential impediments on days when nothing does move.

If teams struggle to think of tasks in the planning meeting, they should consider creating tasks dynamically throughout the sprint. So, as they identify what they will be working on in the daily Scrum ("Today, I will be generating the test data"), they can simply add that task right then to the task board. Granted, the team still runs the risk that a PBI was underestimated due to forgotten tasks. But after a couple of sprints of dynamically creating tasks, teams will begin to see patterns and often become progressively better at identifying tasks before commitments have been made.

The Secret Agenda

The Problem

Whether a team uses a physical or electronic task board, the daily Scrum is a logical time to move tasks from "not started" to "in process" to "complete." Many teams that use physical task boards like to do this meeting standing at the board, actually moving tasks as they are giving their updates. Occasionally, a team dutifully stands up to do their daily Scrum but has no interaction with the board whatsoever. This is because none of the work they are doing is described by the tasks on the board. They often report lots of work they have completed since the previous day, but there is just one problem: none of that work has anything to do with the user stories to which they have committed.

Why This Happens

It is possible this situation can arise as an extreme example of Blob tasks. The team may be carrying the entire task list in their heads. However a more common reason for the Secret Agenda is that the team is experiencing impediments. They are performing work that is outside the boundaries of the sprint commitment. A common reason for this is stakeholder interference. Stakeholders who are used to being able to approach individual team members for favors, meaning help whenever they need it, often have a hard time breaking this habit. They may even acknowledge what they are doing, saying, "Hey, I know you are in the middle of a sprint, but could I get you to look at this bug I found really quick?" If team members are used to this behavior from the days before Scrum, it may not register to them as a problem. Therefore, they won't identify it as such in the daily Scrum.

But Secret Agenda tasks are often generated by the team members themselves. Particularly when they are still learning the Scrum framework, they can have a tendency to do this in two key ways. First, they may add more functionality to a given PBI than requested by the Product Owner. Though they may have good intentions, such "gold-plating" usually ends up making the Product Owner unhappy because it means the requirement will be more expensive to produce. Another habit team members may have is building in functionality that is lower in the backlog to avoid visiting a piece of code twice. Their reasoning is, "Hey, I can see I will be back in this area of the code for backlog item number twenty-eight, so I am just going to do both pieces of work now." The danger, of course, is that, because the backlog can be reordered each sprint, PBI number twenty-eight might be moved down or removed completely as the Product Owner gets new information. When team members do this, they run the risk of adding functionality never asked for and to which they have not made a commitment.

The Fix

In all cases, Secret Agenda tasks should be written down and added to the task board. That alone will often be enough to stop team members from doing work that does not contribute directly to a sprint commitment. As soon as the Product Owner sees that team members have been spending time on work that is not part of the sprint commitment, she can have a discussion about why this is happening.

Sometimes team members are being pulled away from work on the sprint to help stakeholders, and neither the Product Owner nor ScrumMaster feels he or she can say no to this particular stakeholder. This is often the case if the interfering party is a manager. When that happens, it can be useful to point out how this extra work is impacting the sprint. Some teams do this by adding a special "user story" to their sprint called "non-sprint work." Then it is easy to see the volume of work being requested that is not part of the sprint commitment. This tool can be used as a conversation opener by the ScrumMaster as she tries to help stakeholders understand the impact they are having on the project.

The Task Purgatory

The Problem

As we said before, it is ideal to keep tasks small—about a day's worth of work or less. The idea behind this is both to make sure tasks are not forgotten and to show progress. Ultimately, a Product Owner is concerned with backlog items rather than tasks being done. In a Product Owner's mind, PBIs live in a very black-or-white state. They are either done or not done. There is no such thing as almost done or partially done. Seeing tasks move to the done column of a task board is not a guarantee that the user story to which they belong is done to the Product Owner's satisfaction. But it is a promising sign and can give the PO a level of comfort about the sprint.

Not surprisingly, then, what can make a Product Owner very nervous is when tasks seem never to move to the done column. Instead, they stack up in the "in process" column until the last day of the sprint when, magically, they seem to move over in droves. Or maybe they don't. That, of course, is the danger. When tasks languish in the "in process" column, they are in Task Purgatory, and the Product Owner can have a poor sense of how the project is going.

Why This Happens

Team members can find themselves with a Task Purgatory for a number of reasons. Though the ScrumMaster's role exists in a large part to remove impediments, sometimes it can be strangely difficult for teams to ask for this help. Team members have a tendency to discuss their progress on a task by saying something like, "I'm still working on it," when in fact they are truly impeded and no longer making forward progress. This can particularly be true when the team member is stuck on a technical problem. Technical professionals pride themselves on their ability to create solutions to problems. Admitting you can't and asking for help can be difficult at first.

Teams may also experience impediments that are outside the boundaries of their control. Having dependencies on outside entities, such as vendors, can leave tasks sitting "in process" until the outside party completes his part of the work.

But often the reason a Task Purgatory develops is that the team members are reluctant to call work done. "Done" sounds very final, and keeping tasks in "in process" is comfortable. It allows more effort to be put into individual tasks if needed. Often team members will prefer to leave tasks in an in-process state until the last day of the sprint "just in case." Unfortunately, this creates a nail-biting situation for the Product Owner. From his perspective, the team is not maintaining transparency in the project, and he has no idea whether or not the sprint commitment will be met.

The Fix

The ScrumMaster and Product Owner both must emphasize the importance of seeing progress in the sprint. The whole idea of having a daily Scrum is to provide visibility into how the sprint is moving along. This meeting's value is severely limited if the team is not being forthcoming about the work. The ScrumMaster should listen to each team member's update and try to pick up clues about impediments that are implied but not explicitly mentioned. For dependencies on external parties, some teams like to add a column to their task boards called "impeded" for tasks that are now outside their control to deliver. Doing this can give the ScrumMaster fuel for discussions when working with those outside parties to figure out how to move forward.

One way to help a team that has a tendency to leave tasks in process until the very end of the sprint is to track progress on their sprint burndown chart by user stories rather than hours of work remaining or tasks. The "in-process-lingerers" will quickly learn that their habit means the burndown looks as if they are making no progress. It can help them understand that this is how it looks to the Product Owner. Experiencing this firsthand can help a team see the importance of showing the true progress of a sprint.

Task creation and completion are important parts of project transparency in Scrum. Teams must remember that, just as they have made commitments to the Product Owner, the Product Owner has taken that information and made commitments of his own, often to management and even to external customers. Helping the Product Owner see the true progress in a sprint, for better or worse, helps him provide appropriate expectations to these external stakeholders and reduces the chance they will start actively interfering with the project to get the answers they seek themselves.

Determining Doneness

Hopefully a sprint progresses as expected with tasks and user stories being moved to the done column on a regular basis. At the end of the iteration, the sprint review is a chance for the Product Owner to formally accept user stories as done. Because the PBIs are demonstrated at a sprint review, stakeholders are often included at this meeting. It is a good time for them to see incremental progress on the project and to give the Product Owner new user stories that may be included in the product backlog.

But ultimately, this meeting is for the Product Owner. He will need to look at each completed user story and either accept or reject it. A story that has been accepted is included in the final product, and no more work is done on it. If a story is rejected, the Product Owner moves it back into the backlog, where it can be prioritized as he wishes.

Sometimes, problems occur in the sprint-review meeting because of confusion about doneness. When that happens, PBIs can move into a gray area where it is unclear if they are accepted or not. When that happens, the Scrum team, Product Owner, and stakeholder can be unclear about the result of the sprint and how to move forward. Common problems with the sprint-review meeting include:

The Bait and Switch

The Problem

A typical sprint-review meeting happens in two parts. First, an overview is given of the work done in the sprint. This discussion will often center on the sprint goal, the high-level objective the sprint was to accomplish. Starting this meeting at a more general level can be helpful to give context to the stakeholders attending, as they are often not as familiar with the project and its day-to-day work as the team and Product Owner.

After this introductory discussion, the team must get more specific. They must present the completed user stories to the Product Owner and ask if they are accepted as done. The typical format for this is as follows: a team member reads the user story and its acceptance criteria. Then the team member demonstrates where in the product those acceptance criteria have been met. This step is to provide evidence to the Product Owner that agreements about doneness have been met. This discussion will conclude with the team member saying something like, "So, based on this, do you accept this user story as done?"

For example:

"As a call center manager, I want to know average telephone queue wait time so I can plan department staffing."

Done when:

- I can see averages by hour of day, day, and week
- I can see number of abandoned calls (caller hangs up) by hour of day, day, and week
- I have exception reports when queue traffic rises above acceptable levels

In this example, the next step would be to demonstrate in the software that these acceptance criteria work and the functionality described in the PBI is complete.

If the user story and acceptance criteria are well written and have been met, it is reasonable for the team to believe the Product Owner will accept the requirement as done. So it is an unpleasant surprise when, even after fulfilling agreements, the Product Owner rejects a story. And even more frustrating when the reason he gives for this is, "Yes, that is what I asked for. But now that I see it, I want something else." In essence, the Product Owner has done a Bait and Switch—asking for one thing but then changing his focus after the fact to another.

Why This Happens

When a Product Owner is still in the early phase of a project, it is not unusual for him to ask for requirements that are later enhanced, revised, or even discarded for a different approach altogether. This is a natural part of the empirical process, discovering the ultimate best form the final product should take. Yet it is both unfair and unnecessary for the Product Owner to allow these discoveries to make him reject user stories. When he does this, he is often thinking in his old, traditional project-management mindset that says, "If I want any more work done on this PBI, I need to reject it so the team will keep working on it." What he fails to realize is that the best way to add richness to a feature is not to keep the user story forever in progress but, instead, to write more user stories with the additional capability. It is quite common for a single feature to be built and enhanced to its final functionality over the course of several user stories. Indeed, most "epic" user stories are broken down and completed in this fashion. Bait and Switch user stories frustrate the team, tend to make user stories impractically large, and set up a sense of distrust between the team and the Product Owner.

The Fix

A Product Owner that creates Bait and Switch PBIs should get into the habit of calling user stories done when the acceptance criteria have been met. Then he can describe additional functionality he desires in future user stories. This helps to keep stories at a granular level and allows many inspect-and-adapt opportunities to discover the final state the feature should take. Remember: doneness in Scrum—especially as the term is used in a sprint-review meeting—is at a PBI level, not a feature level. Ultimately, large features often are created over the course of several user stories. A good Product Owner can separate in his mind these two meanings of "done" and will accept user stories that have met their acceptance criteria, even if he intends to make additional changes to the feature in later sprints.

The Hedge

The Problem

Completing user stories and having them accepted as done by the Product Owner are positive experiences for the team. They give them a sense of accomplishment, knowing they are working their way through the product backlog. Once a user story has been accepted as done by the Product Owner, the team knows that no further work will be done on it. Any additional enhancements to that feature, if desired, will be outlined in additional user stories. In some organizations, particularly those with heavy regulatory requirements, the acceptance of user stories is a fairly formal process. In these instances, an actual sign off may be required on each completed requirement.

In any case, at the end of a sprint-review meeting, the team and Product Owner should clearly understand the state of each PBI from the sprint commitment and whether it was accepted. But sometimes a Product Owner is reluctant to make that call. When asked to accept a user story, he may use terms like:

- "Yeah, that is basically what I wanted. Let's just add Enhancement X, and it will be great."

- "Looks fantastic! Let's put Enhancement Y in it, and that will be even better."

- "Yep—accepted as done! Let's just add a bit more …"

In each case, the Product Owner is implying a user story is done, yet in the same breath, asking for more work on it. He is taking a Hedge position, both stating that he is satisfied with the requirements as they are and holding out for more work to be done.

Why This Happens

A core skill that all Product Owners must have and excel at is the ability to make decisions. The Product Owner role, by its very nature, is a "decider" role. But not everyone who comes to the position is good at that in the beginning. Just as during the sprint, the team can have a tendency to want to not call PBIs done "just in case," the Product Owner can fall prey to this behavior as well. In his mind, if there is any chance he might want additional work done on the feature, he too may have a tendency to hold back on giving an unequivocal thumbs-up on the doneness of a story.

But quite often, when a Product Owner makes the remarks above, he is doing it unconsciously. He does not even realize he is hedging. In his mind, he is only thinking out loud about how to get the most out of a given story.

The Fix

Ultimately, Product Owners must decide: is the PBI done? If the answer is, "Yes, but the feature itself still needs more functionality," then those enhancements must be described in additional user stories.

For example, in the first bullet above, the Product Owner could have said, "Yeah, that is basically what I wanted so I accept this story as done. Just to let you know, I also want Enhancement X, but I will put that into a different user story to be completed in the next sprint." The Product Owner accepts the team's work, but in his mind, he is already planning additional user stories to enhance this work.

In some organizations that work in heavily regulated fields, the sprint-review meeting and story sign-off are a formal affair, with the Product Owner literally signing off stories as part of the auditing process. Others could take a lesson from them. As we said before, user stories live in a very black-or-white state: they are either done or not done. When the Product Owner uses the Hedge, he confuses the issue and makes it hard for both the team and the organization to understand which user stories are actually completed. Instead, he must choose. He can accept a user story as done and know that no further work will be done on it unless a new story is written. Or he can reject the story and reprioritize it for the next sprint. Either way, at least everyone will be clear about the doneness of the given user story.

The Accused

The Problem

As we saw in the cases above, there are certainly times when the Product Owner unjustly rejects a user story that should be accepted as done. But there are also many times, particularly when everyone is still learning the Scrum process, when a user story legitimately does not meet the definition of done. In these cases, the Product Owner is completely within his rights to reject the story. No team likes having their user stories rejected. But occasionally a team can become defensive about this. They try to browbeat the Product Owner into accepting the story. "C'mon—this is basically what you asked for. You should accept it." These situations can devolve into full-on arguments, with both sides more invested in protecting their own ego than understanding if the PBI met the original requirement.

Why This Happens

The most common reason for a PBI to legitimately be rejected is that some of the acceptance criteria were missed. This happens frequently when teams and Product Owners are new to Scrum. In the past, teams may have used task completion as a sign that a requirement was done. If all the tasks that go into a particular requirement are done, then surely that requirement must be done, right?

WEEK 2

Not necessarily. Tasks are a description of the work needed to meet all the acceptance criteria of a given story. If, during the task creation, one of those acceptance criteria is missed, then the task list does not reflect the true total package of the work to be done. The team is set up to fail because their task list does not reflect the total body of work needed to be completed to call a story done.

The Fix

As the team translates user stories into tasks in the sprint-planning meeting, they must have a strong awareness of the acceptance criteria of each story. Though there may not be a one-to-one correlation, acceptance criteria are often the starting point for the testers to begin creating their test plans and scripts. So it is natural that developers should rely heavily on acceptance criteria to know if they are meeting the actual requirement.

It can also be useful for the team to include a step called "verify" in the definition of "done" for all user stories. What they are verifying, in this case, is that all acceptance criteria have been met. This helps ensure that, even when all tasks have been completed, the team takes the extra step of making sure those tasks met the acceptance criteria of the PBI. Some teams choose to include a column in their task boards for the verify activity.

But regardless, teams must remember that it is ultimately the Product Owner's call. He is perfectly within his rights to reject a story if acceptance criteria are missed. Granted, it can be an unpleasant experience for the team to have this happen in the front of a room full of people. But some of our best learning opportunities come from unpleasant experiences. In future sprints, the team will be more careful to check that specific acceptance criteria have been met and the overall quality and predictability of sprints will improve.

Having a good definition of "done" for each PBI helps both the Product Owner and Scrum team. When both sides have clear agreement on what is required to call a story done, there are far fewer unpleasant surprises in the sprint-review meeting as stories the team considered done are rejected. Ultimately, Product Owners and teams want the same thing—to fulfill user stories in a way that creates high-quality, useful functionality. One of the best ways to do that is to have clear agreement on definitions of done for each user story and to stay very aware of those criteria throughout the course of the sprint.

Week 3 – Anatomy of a Sprint

In Week 3 we'll learn how to hold effective Scrum meetings. We'll learn the purpose of each meeting—what it must produce—as well as how to make the time spent in these meetings more productive.

Does this sound familiar?

1. Our teams are starting to dislike Scrum because they feel that they spend all their time in meetings.

2. We spend much of our sprint-planning meetings helping the Product Owner groom the product backlog.

3. We often get to the end of a sprint-planning meeting and still have not made a sprint commitment.

4. Our teams hate the daily Scrum. They say it makes them feel micromanaged.

5. We know our daily Scrums are only supposed to last fifteen minutes, but often they drag on for twice that long.

6. We have a hard time getting everyone to show up on time (or at all!) to our daily Scrums.

7. We like to invite stakeholders to the sprint review so they can see the progress we've made in the sprint. But sometimes they take over the meeting and start pushing their own agendas.

8. Rather than showing working product in the sprint review, we show a PowerPoint presentation of what we've been working on.

9. Management likes to use the sprint retrospective to tell the team what they did wrong in the sprint and demand to know how they will fix these problems in the future.

10. We never seem to get any truly good ideas for improving the process from our retrospectives.

In principle, the Scrum meetings are quite easy to explain. They can each be described in terms of two factors: what they must produce—their outcome—and how they go about producing that outcome. Here are the Scrum meetings, described in such terms:

Meeting	Outcome	Activities
Sprint Planning	A sprint goal or commitment	Determining acceptance criteria, estimating, creating tasks, planning
Daily Scrum	Work coordination	Share progress, raise impediments, identify dependencies
Sprint Review	Agreement on doneness	Present completed user stories, show where/how acceptance criteria have been met, Product Owner accepts or rejects each story, give stakeholders an update on project progress
Sprint Retrospective	Process improvement	Review things that did and did not go well in the sprint, determine what changes in the process to implement in the next sprint

Presented this way, the Scrum meetings seem straightforward and simple. But, like many simple things, the devil is in the details and in the doing, and all these meetings have the potential to go awry. When that happens, their outputs are also compromised. Let's look at them one at a time.

Sprint Planning

The Product Owner comes into a sprint-planning meeting with one desire: to get a commitment from the team to deliver a given number of PBIs in the sprint. Hopefully (from his perspective), that number is big. So the pressure is on the team. Not surprisingly, the team is concerned with getting enough detail about the PBIs such that they can make commitments with confidence. A good sprint-planning meeting is a bit like a dance. The Product Owner wants more items on the "committed" list and will push on the team to that end. But the team pushes back, insistent on getting enough detail to make an intelligent and informed decision before making any promises. And, as with a dance, when each side does its part well, it works with seeming effortlessness. When one or both sides are lacking in skill or execution, the entire effort suffers. Some common problems with sprint-planning meetings are described below.

The 52-card Pick Up

The Problem

In a sprint-planning meeting, the pressure is on the team. They are the ones being asked to make a commitment. So naturally, they will need to spend most of the planning meeting in activities that help them do this: clarifying requirements, estimating, creating tasks, and so forth. These activities can be quite time-consuming, and they will need the bulk of the planning meeting to do them.

So imagine their frustration when a Product Owner sits down in a planning meeting and says, "Well, here is the backlog. Now, it is not in priority order yet because I haven't had any time to work on this since last sprint. Why don't we take a few minutes now to get it organized?" Instead of coming into this meeting with a well-groomed and prioritized backlog, the Product Owner presents a mish-mash of requirements. He uses time the team needs for other activities (that will get them to a sprint commitment) to groom his backlog. And far from taking "a few minutes," cleaning up and ordering a messy backlog is a little like picking up a deck of cards someone has tossed in the air. It is an activity that can easily expand to take the whole planning meeting.

Why This Happens

Product Owners have an obligation to come to the sprint-planning meeting with a groomed, ordered backlog. "Groomed," in this case, means the PBIs are well-written, of reasonable size (i.e., a few days' work, not a few weeks'), and in the order in which the Product Owner would like them created. In general, as the Product Owner gains more experience and also learns more about the project, the quality of the backlog improves. If this does not happen, it is generally for one reason: he is not putting enough time into backlog maintenance.

The more subtle question is: why is he not giving backlog grooming the time it deserves and needs? It may be because the Product Owner sees the role as a part-time job to be done in his spare time. Consequently, he doesn't have a realistic expectation about how much effort the role takes. He may also be unsure about how to do activities like break down large user stories into more manageable chunks. By bringing such PBIs to the planning meeting, he more or less forces the team to help him with that activity. Finally, a Product Owner with a background of managing projects with the waterfall approach may not be used to listing requirements in the order in which he would like them built. He may be more used to giving the team a requirements document and letting them figure out which items should be built first.

The Fix

There is nothing wrong with the Product Owner wanting and needing the team's help in grooming the backlog. But the sprint-planning meeting is not the right forum for that work. A backlog-grooming meeting or Story-Time session, however, is perfect for such activities. By doing regular Story-Time sessions with the team, and even including stakeholders when needed, the Product Owner gets the help he needs in refining the backlog without taking time the team needs for sprint commitment. Story-Time sessions are not only of benefit to the Product Owner. They are also ideal times for the team to see new user stories that have been added to the backlog. Away from the pressure of planning, the conversations can be more relaxed, and the team, Product Owner, and stakeholders (with the help of the ScrumMaster as facilitator) can work together to prepare the backlog for the next sprint.

A good rule of thumb is to hold a Story-Time session of about sixty to ninety minutes every sprint until it is no longer needed. The meeting should be held a few days before sprint planning, with the idea that the backlog will change very little between this meeting and the planning meeting. Story-Time meetings are crucial early in the project, when emerging requirements are being discovered at a rapid pace. As this stream of changes and additions slows, the Story-Time meeting can be reduced in time or eliminated altogether.

The Extension Filers

The Problem

Using time effectively in a sprint-planning meeting is harder than it might seem at first glance. The team must achieve a balance: they must gain enough detail that they understand the work being requested but not get so lost in the details that they don't discuss enough of the backlog to make a sprint commitment. Experienced Scrum teams get just enough detail in sprint planning to make a commitment, knowing they can fill in the blanks later.

> **Agile Tip**
>
> Holding regular Story-time meetings will make for smoother, more effective, and often shorter sprint-planning sessions.

WEEK 3

It is not unusual for a Scrum team to struggle with this in the beginning. After all, they own the "how," meaning the plan for how the user stories will be turned into functionality. It is part of their responsibility to define the tasks and activities that will eventually fulfill user stories, so it is natural that they focus on that. The danger comes when they get too deep into the details. In these cases, the conversation can begin to spin into the weeds. They start to discuss tasks, who will do what, and even outside dependencies before it is even clear if the user story in question will be in the sprint commitment. They get so wrapped up in trying to fill in all the blanks of the first story that their conversations with the Product Owner never make it any further. And, not surprisingly, what may happen is this team gets to the end of their sprint-planning meeting without making a commitment. The team's response to this problem can be very much like people in the United States who get to April 15 and do not yet have their taxes prepared—they want an extension. "We're not ready to make a commitment. Let's just have another meeting tomorrow to finish this up." But the real problem is not that they didn't have enough time to make a sprint commitment. The problem is they have not used that time well. Consequently, adding more time usually just produces more ineffective conversation, and before they know it, the planning meeting has extended from hours to days.

Why This Happens

When teams are still learning the Scrum process, it can be hard for them to know what constitutes "just enough" information for a given user story. Particularly if they are used to getting a specification that tells them exactly what to build and how to build it, understanding only the basics of a user story can leave them feeling uncomfortable and unprepared to make a decision about commitment. Because they have no practice with getting just enough information to start work, knowing they can work out the details later, they feel uncomfortable with the process. Such teams often subliminally try to create a mini-specification for the sprint, asking the Product Owner an exhaustive list of questions about each backlog item. To do this, they delve much further into the details of each backlog item than is necessary for a planning meeting. So it is not surprising they run out of time.

Also, many teams are not used to the concept of working within a time-box. In the past, their customers may have said, "This is what I want. How long will it take to build it?" Making a sprint commitment is essentially the opposite exercise. The Product Owner says, "Our sprint is two weeks long. How many of my backlog items can I get in that time?" Making the mental shift to answer this question can take some practice. When teams don't make this transition easily, it is common that they get to the end of their planning meeting and have no sprint commitment.

The Fix

A ScrumMaster can help a team make better use of planning meetings in two ways. First, she can actively facilitate the planning session. She does not need to direct the team members in how to explore backlog items, but she can offer observations such as, "We've spent twenty minutes on this requirement. Is it, maybe, time to move on?" This simple question can pull a team out of the weeds and help them realize they are not making the best use of their time.

Another useful technique for developing good habits in sprint planning is to schedule only the Product Owner to be there for the first portion of the meeting. For example, in a four-hour planning session, schedule the Product Owner only for the first half. Then, when the team digs too deeply into the details of a single story, the ScrumMaster can say, "That sounds like a 'how' issue. We have our Product Owner here for only the first half of the meeting, so let's focus on working with him to understand what he will need to see in each PBI by the end of the sprint to call it done." Using these techniques will keep the team focused on truly understanding what the Product Owner is asking for before they start delving into what the solution looks like.

But what if, despite using these techniques, the team gets three hours and fifty minutes into a four-hour planning meeting and has still not made a sprint commitment? That simply means they will make their sprint commitment in those last ten minutes. Will they enjoy that experience? No. Will they have confidence in their commitment? Probably not. But the benefit is that they will not develop the habit of asking for an extension of time when what they really need is to learn how to make better use of the time they have.

In this situation, the ScrumMaster should use active facilitation techniques to help with this "quickie commitment." She should start at the top of the backlog and read the first user story, along with any acceptance criteria. Then she should ask, "Is everyone willing to commit to this PBI?" If everyone says yes, then she moves on to the next user story, using the same technique. Eventually she will get to a user story where the team starts to look hesitant or even says, "I don't think we can do that one." At that point, the line is drawn, and everything above is in the sprint commitment. Using this active facilitation technique, it is not unusual for a team that thought it needed another four hours of discussion to come to a sprint commitment in just a few minutes. Considering the backlog items one at a time and in order gives the conversation the structure it needs to happen quickly and even fairly easily.

The Multi-tasking Mess

The Problem

As an agile coach, a common complaint I hear is, "The sprint-planning meeting takes forever! I feel as if, since we started Scrum, I am spending all my time in meetings!" When I am coaching an organization, I often ask to sit in as an observer on planning meetings. Doing so offers me a unique window into not just how well the organization uses time but also how effective—or ineffective—their communication techniques are.

WEEK 3

As I observe the interactions, it often becomes very clear to me why the sprint-planning meeting is a source of pain for the organization. The problem is that no one is giving full attention to the meeting itself. There may be two people arguing heatedly about a given backlog item, another couple engaged in a side conversation that has nothing to do with the work at hand, and a few more bored and checked out, reading email on their phones. When you couple this with people popping in and out of the meeting, as well as inter-ruptions from outsiders ("I need to borrow Susan for five minutes—sorry!"), you have the makings of a poor sprint-planning meeting. Because everyone is distracted and not giving his or her full attention, the meeting tends to drag on, and—surprise!—no one feels ready at the end of the allotted time to make a commitment.

Why This Happens

Many people and organizations pride themselves on their ability to multi-task. But there is ample research out there that shows when people try to divide their attention between too many targets, they end up not focusing effectively on any of them. I am amazed at how often responsible companies that work hard to control costs in other areas will, nevertheless, spend thousands of dollars each year on ineffective meetings. Having seven to eight expensive professionals in a one-hour meeting that accomplishes nothing is a direct cost. The organization has wasted that money just as though they had torn up one-hundred-dollar bills.

These habits are particularly painful in the sprint-planning meeting, where time is limited and therefore must be used with care. The sloppy practice of giving half an ear to the conversation at hand while also checking email, sending instant messages, and chatting with your neighbor about next week's upcoming office party means you are not contributing fully to the process. As with the Extension Filers, rather than adding more time to the meeting, what is needed is to use the time available more effectively.

The Fix

The ScrumMaster should set the tone for the sprint-planning meeting. She should request everyone's full attention during the meeting so it can be fin-ished as quickly as possible. It is a good idea to have a "no laptops/phones" rule for planning meetings. Taking away these means of distraction often forces people to pay attention by default. Another useful rule is "one person talking at a time." This eliminates side conversations and allows everyone to hear what is being said. Many people find background noise incredibly distracting. The ScrumMaster may find that some of those people who were "checked out" before simply couldn't think over the din of multiple conversations. When this distraction is eliminated, they often resume active participation of their own accord.

A note about learning styles: while listening to conversations, some people doodle on a pad of paper. Do not assume this means they are not paying attention. Strong visual learners often need to "defocus" in order to listen to and consider what is being said. If you've ever approached someone with a complicated request and that person was looking down or away while you talked, you were probably working with a visual learner. If the doodlers still participate in the conversation, ask questions, and so forth, the technique is obviously helping, not hurting, their attention.

Finally, the ScrumMaster must keep outsiders away from the planning meeting. A "do not disturb" sign on the door is a good idea, unless it will be willfully ignored. In those cases, try to arrange it so no one but the ScrumMaster, Product Owner, and Scrum team know where the planning meeting is being held. It is not a bad idea, in cases where interruptions happen frequently, to hold a planning meeting off-site. If that is what it takes to give everyone an environment where they can concentrate, then it will be well worth the extra effort.

> **Agile Tip**
>
> Sprint-planning meetings require the full attention of everyone involved. Many teams institute a "no laptop" rule so participants are not distracted by email and other outside concerns.

WEEK 3

Because planning meetings set the tone for the whole sprint, it is important that they run smoothly. It is not unusual for these meetings to take less time as everyone involved becomes more experienced and comfortable with Scrum. A novice team might need a four-hour meeting to plan a two-week sprint. As they gain more experience and familiarity with the backlog, they might need less than half that time. In any case, it should be emphasized that, regardless of the time scheduled for the meeting, when the team reaches sprint commitment and feels they are ready to get started working, the meeting can end.

Daily Scrum

Of all the Scrum meetings, the daily Scrum is the one most likely to be done out-and-out incorrectly. This comes from a lack of understanding about the purpose of the meeting. In a traditional status meeting, team members report progress to some authority figure, often a project manager. But in a daily Scrum, the team members report to each other for the purpose of work coordination. It is their one guaranteed opportunity each day to touch base with each other and plan their work. For example, if I am a developer who is coding a user story and you are a tester, you might naturally want to know from me, "When is this PBI going to be ready to test?" This is the kind of topic discussed in a daily Scrum. The daily Scrum is also the time to raise issues or impediments so the ScrumMaster can help with them. It is important to note that usually these problems are not solved in the daily Scrum. Rather they are brought to the surface so the right people can know about them.

A daily Scrum is short—about fifteen minutes—and quite structured. Team members talk about what they have done since yesterday, what they will be doing today, and any blocking issues they are experiencing. Everyone gets a chance to speak, including the ScrumMaster and Product Owner if they wish and have anything to add. In general, stakeholders are not included in the daily Scrum.

Sounds simple, right? Simple—yes. Easy—no. Here are some of the things that can go wrong with the daily Scrum.

The Masquerade

The Problem

The first indication you might get that a daily Scrum is being done well is that the team members are talking with and looking at each other. A good daily Scrum sounds like a succinct conversation—to the point and full of useful information. In these instances, the ScrumMaster may almost sit in the background, listening for impediments and helping with active facilitation if the conversation wanders.

But often the daily Scrum looks nothing like this. Instead, you may see the team members reporting to the ScrumMaster, telling her what they did yesterday, will do today, and so on. In such cases, there is little to no interaction between team members. And the information being given is not so much about coordinating work as it is about telling the ScrumMaster how time is being spent. Team member updates are often at a very trivial level, just enough to "satisfy" the ScrumMaster that work is actually being done. In these cases, teams are, in fact, not really doing a daily Scrum at all. They are having a status meeting.

Why This Happens

The status meeting masquerading as a daily Scrum often occurs due to old habits. If teams have had to report status to an authority figure in the past, they may find it hard at first to break this habit. It becomes doubly difficult if the person who was once their project manager is now their ScrumMaster. They may be so used to being questioned by this person about how they spent their time and their progress on tasks that they simply continue that communication pattern.

Then, too, the project-manger-turned-ScrumMaster may not realize she is leading the meeting. She may be so used to getting status information from team members that she unconsciously grills them about their progress. Even in her new role as ScrumMaster, she may still feel responsible for the ultimate success or failure of the project. When this happens, she shifts her focus away from facilitating the Scrum process and moves instead towards controlling and directing the team.

The Fix

The first step in correcting this problem is to shift the primary speaking role from the ScrumMaster to the team members. Many ScrumMasters complain, "I take the lead only because my team members would just sit there and say nothing if I didn't." This might be true for a little while. But once team members see the ScrumMaster really isn't in charge of the conversation anymore, they will step in to fill the void. If you are a ScrumMaster who has inadvertently been holding daily Scrum status meetings, try this exercise in your next daily Scrum. Limit your speaking for the entire meeting to this one sentence: "Who wants to start?" If your question is met by silence, so much the better. People become very uncomfortable very quickly in this situation. Someone will speak up, just to break the stillness. And then the meeting can

WEEK 3

start. Once the team realizes you really are going to take a background role, they will have no choice but to start talking to each other.

It can also be helpful in this situation for the ScrumMaster to physically separate herself from the team. For example, if the team does their daily Scrum standing around a task board posted on the wall, she can stand back from them a couple feet. This makes it harder for team members to speak directly to her (some would have to turn 180 degrees to do this), so they naturally look at the task board and each other. If the ScrumMaster wants to interject a comment or question, she can move forward. Then, when finished, she should resume her position slightly outside the team.

The DMV

The Problem

When organizations complain that doing Scrum seems to mean sitting in meetings all day, one of the first things I enquire about is how much time it takes to do the average daily Scrum. The answer should be near that fifteen-minute goal. One company I worked with detested doing daily Scrums. When I came onsite to help them, I found out why: their daily Scrums were averaging an hour each! Just about anyone would come to dislike Scrum if they had that experience. Long, drawn-out daily Scrums can make a team that was initially excited about Scrum quickly long for the good old days when all they had to do was show up for a weekly status meeting. Sitting in a daily Scrum for an hour a day every day is about as much fun as spending a Saturday morning sitting in the DVM, waiting to renew your driver's license.

> ## Agile Tip
>
> The mark of an effective daily Scrum is that the team members talk primarily to each other, not to their ScrumMaster. A good daily Scrum is like a succinct conversation—to the point and filled with useful information.

Why This Happens

There are a couple common reasons a daily Scrum extends well beyond its normal time range. The first is people coming in late. Think about it: if you miss five minutes of a daily Scrum, you missed a third of the meeting. Often the team will start over when the late person arrives and repeat information he missed. When several people are late, this can quickly double the length of the meeting.

Another reason for a lengthy daily Scrum is allowing too many sidebar conversations—ones that either are not of immediate pressing importance or are of interest mainly to a limited number of people. For example, if you and I need to come up with a strategy for generating test data, why should we make the rest of our team sit there while we discuss this? Far better to say something like, "Let's get together after the daily Scrum and work this out." Doing this shows respect for the rest of the team's time. Every team member should feel comfortable speaking up to say, "Hey, that sounds like a sidebar issue. Can you guys take that up after the daily Scrum?" At first, it may be only the ScrumMaster doing this. But ideally, the team will police each other on this issue and make certain their daily Scrum time is being well spent.

The Fix

Every team member needs to make a commitment to be at the daily Scrum every day and to show up on time. One great way to help this along is to allow the team members, as opposed to the ScrumMaster, to choose the time of day to hold the meeting. Maybe you don't have a team of early birds. Or maybe you live in an area where morning traffic is unpredictable. In these situations, an 8 a.m. daily Scrum time might not work. Implicit in letting the team choose the time is that they have agreed on the ideal time for this meeting and, therefore, will show up for it on time and ready to go. An observation: while there is no perfect time to do a daily Scrum, the ones I've done that were scheduled for 11:45 a.m. invariably ended on time. Everyone was anxious to finish up and go to lunch!

Sidebar conversations can easily double or triple the length of a daily Scrum, so they must be dealt with effectively. One approach is to reserve the daily Scrum meeting room for an hour, even though the scheduled meeting time is much shorter. That makes it easy to say, "Why don't you guys hang around after the meeting and discuss that between yourselves?"

WEEK 3

Squeaky Rats

Scrum teams can find playful, inventive ways to enforce the no-sidebar-conversation rule. Some keep a number of squeaky toys shaped like rats on the table in the team room. When anyone thinks the conversation is "going down a rathole"—i.e., getting too far into the details or off-topic—she can squeak a rat as a gentle reminder to her teammates to curtail their discussion until later.

The Dabbler

The Problem

As we have emphasized before, the value of the daily Scrum is that it is the one time each day all team members are guaranteed to be together. Sometimes Scrum novices don't see the value in that daily inspect-and-adapt point. "We sit by each other and can talk any time. So a daily meeting is a waste," they may say. Or they may have experienced long daily Scrum meetings as described above and think a solution would be limiting not the length of the daily Scrum but the frequency of the meetings. Finally, some Scrum team members feel they can drop in to the daily Scrum when they feel like it. When it is not convenient for them to attend, they simply skip the meeting altogether. In each of these cases, team members not only fail to see the benefit of the daily Scrum but also lack understanding about how skipping this meeting impairs Scrum itself. Instead, they dabble at doing Scrum in a part-time manner, never truly embracing the empirical process or gaining the benefits it has to offer.

Why This Happens

When organizations reduce the frequency of their daily Scrum, it tells me they do not really understand the purpose of the meeting. The daily Scrum is not a meeting used to work out problems but rather to assess and, if necessary, correct the course of the sprint. Each day of a sprint, the Scrum team, ScrumMaster, and Product Owner have in their minds a game plan for the remaining days of the sprint. The daily Scrum is a touchpoint to discover if that game plan needs to be adjusted. Teams are absolutely right that, if they need to check in with each other or have questions throughout the day they can do so in a spontaneous way as needed. But these conversations are simply refinements of the "how," meaning how individual elements of the sprint commitment are to be delivered. But corrections to the overall approach of a sprint must happen with the whole team present, as well as the ScrumMaster and especially the Product Owner. A good daily Scrum is rather like a football team's huddle: a quick but vital touchpoint to make sure everyone knows the game plan and his or her role in it.

The Fix

Daily attendance at this meeting is part of doing Scrum. The ScrumMaster should emphasize this to team members. It is also helpful to have the Product Owner regularly attend the daily Scrum. With their "customer" present, it is sometimes easier for team members to see why it is important for everyone to hear the same information. When a Product Owner takes his turn to speak in the daily Scrum, he often spends that time asking clarifying questions about what the team members have discussed. It would be much more time consuming and ineffective if the Product Owner had to follow up with each team member individually. And if, on a given day, there is very little change to report, that simply means the daily Scrum can be very short. A quick update ensures everyone knows the status of the sprint and any issues or concerns that need attention.

The daily Scrum is a vital part of the inspect-and-adapt process. Teams should aim to keep their daily Scrums brief but content-rich. Everyone—the Scrum team, ScrumMaster, and Product Owner—should leave this meeting feeling he or she has a good understanding of both the overall health of the sprint and the activities for the day. Having this common knowledge is a key point of transparency in Scrum.

Sprint Review

The sprint-review meeting has two purposes. Its primary purpose is to gain agreement on doneness. The Scrum team has a number of user stories, which they consider done. Now it is time to see if the Product Owner agrees. In some organizations, the Product Owner actually signs off each PBI as it is accepted. In other cases, a verbal acceptance is the norm. But regardless of the level of formality, the process is the same. The presenting team member

WEEK 3

reads the first user story, along with its acceptance criteria. He then shows the Product Owner where in the product those acceptance criteria have been fulfilled. In essence, he is giving the Product Owner evidence that he should accept the story as done. If the Product Owner believes the acceptance criteria have been met, he will accept the story. If he feels some acceptance criteria have been missed, he may reject the story and ask the team to do more work on it in the next sprint. This presenting of the evidence happens for each completed user story.

The secondary purpose of the sprint-review meeting is to allow stakeholders to see progress. It is up to the Product Owner to decide which stakeholders should attend. They may be customers, subject-matter experts, management, or other individuals who have a strong vested interest in the product. These periodic glimpses into the progress being made go a long way towards making stakeholders feel involved with the work being done. In a more traditional waterfall-style product development, the stakeholders often go months without getting any real sense of how their project is going. With Scrum, they can get that information at the end of each sprint.

But, as with all Scrum meetings, the sprint review can sometimes go awry. Below are some common problems with this meeting.

The Blue Screen of Death

The Problem

Over time, the Scrum inner circle (the Scrum team, ScrumMaster, and Product Owner) often grow quite comfortable with one another. Because so often they have to talk about problems and issues within a sprint, these kinds of conversations that air dirty laundry are quite commonplace. But when stakeholders are involved, the dynamic changes. These individuals are not so involved in the day-to-day workings of the sprint. They usually do not have the same level of trust in the process as the Scrum inner circle, which has seen solutions as well as problems as the team has progressed. Therefore, care should be taken that the sprint review is a positive experience for them. When technical issues, system crashes, or negative conversations arise between the team and Product Owner, stakeholders can get the impression the project is not going well. If a team member is demonstrating the working functionality of the sprint, only to have the entire system crash, that is not likely to inspire confidence in a stakeholder's mind that the project is going well.

Why This Happens

There is no need to turn the sprint review into a major stage production, with days of preparation. But everyone should realize that having stakeholders in the rooms ups the ante a bit. Ironically, because the ScrumMaster and Product Owner are so effective at insulating them from the "chickens," Scrum team members can forget how important it is that these people feel positive about the project. In some cases, they are the individuals actually funding the project. Continued support for work can hinge on their impressions during the sprint review. So showing the project in its best possible light is in everyone's benefit.

Then, too, what is being demonstrated in a sprint review should never come as a complete surprise to the Product Owner when stakeholders are attending. If it does, that is an indication he has not been involved enough during the sprint itself. It is the Product Owner's job to manage stakeholder expectations. He cannot do that if he has no sense of what victories (completed PBIs) and disappointments (things that were missed or remain unfinished) will be presented in this meeting.

The Fix

When important stakeholders are attending the sprint review, teams should allow time for a "dress rehearsal." This practice session can be brief, but the team should make sure—using the same computer they will use for the actual sprint review—that all functionality, test data, and examples are working as expected. They should also decide at this time who will present which user stories. Some teams like to have the person who developed a story present it. Other times, they may want the ScrumMaster to present. Obviously, personal preference should be taken into account here. Some developers enjoy the pride of ownership that comes from showing off something they had a hand in designing and building. But if someone is deathly shy, don't force the issue. The most important thing is to have this worked out ahead of time so transitions can be smooth.

Also, when stakes are high, the Product Owner should know ahead of time any bad news that will be conveyed in the sprint review so he can begin active expectation management with key stakeholders. No one likes to hear a team committed to eight PBIs will actually deliver only half that many. But if the Product Owner knows this ahead of time, he can prep stakeholders so this information doesn't come as a surprise.

The Hostile Takeover

The Problem

In addition to demonstrating functionality, the sprint-review meeting can be a natural time to gather feedback from stakeholders. Particularly for geographically dispersed groups, this meeting may be the only time outsiders get together to view the work in progress. Indeed, some teams schedule a combined sprint review/Story-Time meeting—for example, following the review with a backlog-grooming session—to take advantage of having so many people from whom they need feedback in one place.

But sometimes stakeholders have their own agenda. Rather than give specific feedback and answer questions, unruly stakeholders can sometimes take over a sprint-review meeting. They can launch into questions, side topics, and other kinds of discussions that pull the meeting away from its purpose. They can also begin giving the team specific direction ("In the next sprint-review meeting, I want to see X"), forgetting that it is the Product Owner who will decide the priorities of future sprints. When this happens, the sprint review has been derailed from its original purpose. At its worst, this kind of Hostile Takeover can turn a sprint-review meeting into total chaos, with the stakeholders running the show and no agreement on doneness being achieved.

> ### Agile Tip
>
> While the sprint review is the formal time for declaring work done, Product Owners and teams can meet throughout the sprint to review backlog items. Indeed, this is the preferred approach when important stakeholders, such as outside clients, will be attending the review.

Why This Happens

Stakeholders often do not have the same level of experience with Scrum as the team members, ScrumMaster, or Product Owner. Therefore, they may not yet have good Scrum manners, meaning they may not know what is and is not appropriate behavior in this meeting. Being unfamiliar with working within a timebox, they may be more used to traditional meetings where the discussion is allowed to wander into sidebars and other non-productive paths.

Then, too, they may view this meeting as their one chance to give feedback. In their enthusiasm to make sure their requirements get into the product backlog, they may unconsciously dominate the conversation. When others disagree with their requests, this can easily spiral into lengthy discussions and arguments.

Finally, a common reason for a Hostile Takeover in a sprint-review meeting is that there are simply too many stakeholders present. Inviting twenty stakeholders to a sprint-review meeting is asking for trouble. There are too many lines of communication, and a chaotic meeting is almost always the result.

The Fix

If it seems stakeholders are staging a hostile takeover of the sprint-review meeting, the ScrumMaster must step in. This is the chance for her active facilitation skills to shine. She should listen for the conversation veering off course and gently but firmly steer it back on track. If the team is employing the combo sprint review/Story-Time meeting, one way to do this is to say, "That sounds like an important requirement. Let's make sure we capture it in Story-Time, but for now, let's finish the sprint review."

> **Agile Tip**
>
> The Product Owner should have final say over which stakeholders are invited to the sprint review.

WEEK 3

Another helpful technique to use when several people are talking at once is to look at and speak to only the Product Owner. For example, if two stakeholders are having an argument about how a particular feature should work, the Scrum-Master can ask the Product Owner, "How do you see this feature working?" By doing this, she essentially refocuses the conversation on the Product Owner and subtly reminds stakeholders of his importance.

Finally, be wary of inviting too many stakeholders to a sprint-review meeting. As with Story-Time meetings, it is better to hold multiple sessions with smaller groups than one large meeting. In general, do not let stakeholders outnumber the Scrum inner circle. And remember that the larger the group, the more active and firm role a ScrumMaster will need to take in facilitation.

The Body Double

The Problem

We've said that, during the sprint-review meeting, the team must give the Product Owner evidence that he should accept the completed user stories as done. The primary way this is accomplished is by showing the working functionality. For example, look at the following user story:

> "As a customer service representative, I can log notes from a customer call."

Acceptance Criteria:

- Max of 256 characters
- Can attach other documents via link
- Searchable by date
- Optional red-flag status to indicate serious issue
- Searchable by red-flag status

The way a Scrum team would demonstrate this user story as done is by showing the feature itself and how the acceptance criteria has been fulfilled. For example, they may try to enter more than 256 characters and show how that attempt is not successful. They may demonstrate adding a "red flag" and searching on red-flag comments. In each case, the best evidence that they have done as the Product Owner asked is to show working functionality.

But some teams do not show working features in their sprint-review meetings. Instead, they present a PowerPoint of what they've been working on. This presentation may be very convincing and allude to all kinds of advancements in the product. But, as with a Body Double in the movies, looks can be deceiving. The Product Owner may not be seeing his real user story fulfilled at all but rather a picture of something that looks like it. Pretty screen shots in a presentation might dazzle an inexperienced stakeholder, but a Product Owner knows better. Any use of the Body-Double presentation, without accompanying real working examples, should be met with suspicion by the Product Owner.

Why This Happens

One of the most common reasons—and most troublesome—that a team might use a PowerPoint for their sprint review is that the PBIs to which they committed are, in fact, not done. The team may feel they are almost done or more or less done. In their minds, they feel this is as good as done. But, in the Product Owner's mind, such backlog items are not, in fact, done. "Done" in a Product Owner's mind means the functionality described in the user story works, fulfillment of the acceptance criteria can be demonstrated, and the feature could be released to customers right away if desired. If the team had really completed these steps, they could demonstrate them in the working software. Because they choose instead to show a picture of the feature, the Product Owner can assume the real feature is not done and should be rejected.

But sometimes teams will legitimately struggle with how to show that a given user story is done. This can happen in non-user-interface-intensive projects, such as embedded software. When there is no UI involved, it can be challenging to show, for example, that a validation passed from one part of the system to another. In an effort to give the Product Owner evidence the user story has been fulfilled, the team may resort to a description in a presentation of the work they did. But this approach still gives the Product Owner no real information or evidence that the user story has been fulfilled. The team, in essence, is asking him to take their word for it.

The Fix

Product Owners should make it very clear they will accept no feature as done until they can see evidence it works as agreed upon. Any tendency to resort to PowerPoint presentations in a sprint review is a habit that should be nipped in the bud. Both the Product Owner and ScrumMaster should reinforce that what should be shown in the sprint review is working features, not screen shots. If a feature has no user interface from which to demonstrate that it works, the team will have to get a bit more clever. They need to give the Product Owner some evidence that the feature works as promised. Sometimes, they can share test results. Some examples of this kind of demonstration would be showing that a data element successfully passed from one

WEEK 3

system to another or that a load test for a specific number of users passed. In each case, there is no specific user interface to demonstrate, but the team still gives the Product Owner evidence that his feature works as planned.

Many organizations find that, from the viewpoint of the Product Owner and stakeholders, regular sprint reviews are the single biggest benefit of Scrum. Whereas in traditional development they may have had to wait months for a glimpse of the product, now they can see new functionality up and working at the end of every sprint. Instead of getting vague status reports about development being "74 percent complete," they now can hear in each sprint how many features are complete. This is often viewed—rightly so—as much more concrete feedback. So teams, ScrumMasters, and Product Owners should work together to make the sprint review a positive experience for everyone involved.

Sprint Retrospective

The purpose of the retrospective is improvement in the sprint process. It is primarily for the team to talk about their processes and how well they do or do not work. It is also a time to talk about things that went amiss in the sprint. Estimations that were wildly wrong, sprint commitments that were not met—these are typical conversations in a sprint retrospective. Because, to an extent, this meeting is about airing dirty laundry, it requires both a high level of trust and honesty to truly be effective. When those elements are missing, these problems can occur.

The Inquisition

The Problem

It is never fun to talk about what you did wrong. But the empirical process requires analyzing results—good or bad—with the idea of making incremental improvements in later sprints. In practice, doing this is easiest when the people involved feel emotionally safe. When the Scrum inner circle develops strong trust between its members, these discussions can happen in a frank and productive way. But when the trust is lacking or outsiders are included in the retrospective, that level of emotional safety can drop dramatically. At its worst, this situation can devolve into an inquisition of the team, where they are forced to defend their actions or explain how they are going to do better next time or both. When this happens, the team justifiably feels under attack. They shift their thinking from "What can we do better next time?" to "How can we get out of this alive?" At that point, an us-against-them attitude has developed, and any opportunities for brainstorming future improvements are shut down.

Why This Happens

With the exception of the sprint review, stakeholders are not generally helpful additions to the Scrum meetings. But nowhere is their presence more damaging than in the retrospective. Because of the nature of the meeting and the exposure of the good, bad, and ugly of the sprint, the teams are in an especially vulnerable position. They would like to use the retrospective to improve their working processes. But stakeholders have their own agendas and desires. They may be less concerned with improving the overall process and more focused on why they didn't get their particular backlog items delivered in the last sprint. At worst, they berate the team and want to know how they are going to fix things in the next sprint. When this kind of feedback comes from a powerful stakeholder, such as a manager, the team's survival instincts will kick in. They will shift their thinking and conversation away from sharing ideas and towards defending themselves. They may even shut down completely and sit in stony silence while stakeholders rail on about their failings and how they must do better next time.

The Fix

The ScrumMaster must do everything in her power to create a safe, open environment for the retrospective. Banning stakeholders from this meeting is a great first step. The ScrumMaster's and Product Owner's roles exist in large part to shield the team from negative interactions like these from stakeholders. This is their opportunity to step up and make certain the team is protected from outsiders.

ScrumMasters and Product Owners should also carefully monitor their own behavior in this

WEEK 3

Agile Tip

The nature of a sprint retrospective requires a safe environment in which to talk about problems in the sprint and other dirty laundry. Of all the Scrum meetings, this one is most impaired by any lack of trust, for example, if stakeholders are present.

meeting to ensure they are not subconsciously acting as Inquisitors. This can be challenging. Because of their place in the Scrum inner circle, they do have a right to make observations and ask questions. A Product Owner is within his rights to say, "Last sprint we committed to ten user stories but only delivered three. What happened?" The difference, however, is in the delivery of and intent behind the question. Whereas stakeholders, being outsiders, often lapse into "you" statements ("You did this wrong" or "You didn't give me the PBIs I wanted") the ScrumMaster and Product Owner should speak in terms of "we" and really mean it. Maybe the reason the team missed their commitment is that the Product Owner did not give good clarity on acceptance criteria. A feeling of "we are all in this together and all want to work to improve the process" will go a long way towards making the retrospective a positive interaction where open and honest communication can occur.

The Poker Tournament

The Problem

As we have said, one of the most important elements of a successful retrospective is a sense of open communication. One big step towards creating such an environment is to exclude outsiders from this meeting. But what happens when the Scrum inner circle itself lacks trust? What if the Scrum team members do not trust each other or feel comfortable communicating in an honest way? In practice, this problem is even more damaging to the retrospective than having outside Inquisitors berate the team. At least, in that situation, the Scrum team feels a sense of camaraderie with their fellow teammates as they defend themselves against outside criticism. But when the team members lack trust in each other, no real sense of team exists. It becomes every man for himself.

Though these meetings can sometimes be marked by hostile conversation, often the very opposite is true. Retrospectives among team members who do not trust each other are often an exercise in revealing as little as possible. Their communication is cagey, and any feedback they offer is usually at a very trivial level. They may insist they have no suggestions for improvements because "everything is fine." Their goal becomes not so much improving the process but getting out of the meeting without revealing any information that will lead to uncomfortable conversations. Much like professional poker players, they think of their teammates more as adversaries than partners.

Why This Happens

Scrum teams may lack trust if they do not yet know each other well. But the intense nature and shared experiences of working on a Scrum team should remedy this problem within a sprint or two. Scrum team members may or may not become best friends. But they do often develop their own internal culture, language, and sense of tribe. For example, many Scrum teams have team names or nicknames for people on the team. These adopted names are often private jokes where only the team members know the origins. A seemingly silly behavior like this is actually a strong indication of team bonding. It means the team has developed a sense of "we." When this kind of bonding doesn't occur, the communication in the team rarely progresses to the level of honesty required to speak frankly about problems.

Other times, Scrum teams suffer from lack of trust because the organization has strict hierarchies and the team is made up of members who cross those hierarchical boundaries. A team of three software developers, two testers, and two user-interface designers may actually be three sub-teams, divided across function. Within their own function, there is trust. But there is no such trust in the "other guys." To the contrary, they may see these people as the cause of all the problems in the project. But rather than directly challenge them, they take a "don't make waves" attitude.

Finally, Scrum teams that lack good communication may feel there is an implied class structure in the organization. If the team is comprised of some members who are considered less important than others, this can strongly inhibit communication. Interestingly, this often has less to do with technical skill and more to do with things like tenure. A newly hired team member may be extremely technically adept. But his suggestions for improvements are often met directly or indirectly with the response of "You don't understand how we do thing around here." After a couple of episodes of this feedback, the snubbed team member learns to avoid any further suggestions and just go along with what others want.

WEEK 3

The Fix

If the ScrumMaster senses the communication at the retrospective lacks true openness, she must do what she can to guide the conversation to a deeper level. It is not usual for team members to come to the ScrumMaster privately to vent their frustrations. When this happens, she should encourage them to bring these issues forward in the retrospective. In the beginning, it may be easier for her to be the one to raise these issues. She can provide the opening in the conversation to expose an issue and invite team members to comment on it. This middleman position is not ideal. Eventually, it is better to have team members who can speak their minds. But in the beginning when trust is developing, it is a reasonable step towards that end goal.

Ironically one of the simplest and most effective ways to break a team communication pattern of stiff, stilted conversation is to occasionally hold the retrospective off-site. People develop a work persona, a way of behaving in their professional environment. Simply removing them from the familiar work environment can change their attitude and behavior. Perhaps at one time you've had a co-worker whom you didn't know well but then encountered in a social situation. After spending time with him in this different environment, you may have thought, "Wow—I didn't realize he was such a cool guy."

Getting away from the confining, beige walls of a conference room can do wonders for setting people at ease. Go to a local restaurant, pub, or café. Get everyone a bite to eat and their favorite beverage. Then have your retrospective. You will be amazed at the change in dynamic. When people have a chance to relax and feel comfortable, the level of communication can improve dramatically.

The Complainer's Forum

The Problem

Since the retrospective focuses on improving the process, it is a natural forum for raising impediments. Some of these issues are things over which the team has influence. But often they stem from outside entities. For example, teams may have dependencies on external groups that interfere with their ability to deliver on commitments. Such impediments will often require the help of the ScrumMaster and other outside parties to resolve.

It is expected that the issues raised in the retrospective will be a mix of things over which the team has influence and those which they do not. But when the problems being raised are exclusively outside the scope of the team's ability to fix, a closer look is required. It is possible to have a situation where a team has ideal processes but outside influences make it hard for them execute those processes. But, more often, hearing a litany of issues that are all outside a team's control can be a sign that the team is misusing the retrospective. Rather than using the meeting to evaluate their own work and how they can improve it, they externalize their problems and use the time to hold a complaint session. Their focus is less concerned with how they can change their own behaviors and more about how everyone else is making their lives harder. Teams may even take a "victim" attitude, insisting their project would run like a well-oiled machine if it weren't for "those other guys." In such situations, the ScrumMaster will hear only complaints and suggestions for others changing their behavior, never anything that team members themselves will change or improve.

Why This Happens

Retrospectives can turn into complaint sessions because teams don't understand the real purpose of the meeting. When they hear, "We are going to talk about what went well in the sprint and what didn't go so well," they may equate this with the "lessons learned" meeting of traditional project management. Typically done at the end of an entire project, the lessons-learned meeting is designed to capture what did and did not go well in the project with the idea of applying this to future projects. In practice, this forward application hardly ever happens. Projects differ from each other in scope, requirements, and the people involved. The lessons learned from one project may not be applicable to another.

With the retrospective, our improvements are all within the same project and targeted specifically to the next sprint. They are not captured with the idea of using them at some far-off future date but starting tomorrow, when the next sprint begins. Suppose you take up the sport of golf and begin taking lessons. You are at the driving range hitting balls. As you get feedback from your instructor about your golf swing, you don't usually think, "That is a great idea. Maybe I will think about doing that someday, and maybe I could even apply that advice to tennis too." Instead, you realize this information is situation-specific, and you try to incorporate his feedback the very next time you hit the ball.

When teams can identify improvements that involve only others, rather than themselves, making changes, it may indicate a reluctance to use the retrospective for its true purpose. The idea that "my life would be perfect if Person A and Person B made these changes" indicates someone who may be uncomfortable with introspection. Team members may also have the idea that identifying areas to improve means something was wrong with their original process. Instead of viewing how they do their work as an ever-changing, ever-adapting process, they see it as a black-or-white, right-or-wrong proposition. Teams that feel this way often believe that if they admit any need for improvement they are tacitly saying they were in the wrong to begin with.

The Fix

In their retrospective, the team should be looking for incremental changes they can introduce right away that may produce an improved process. A good scientist knows that he must limit the number of variables he changes in a given experiment. If too many changes are introduced at once, he has a hard time establishing the connection of the specific cause with the outcome. Likewise, in the retrospective, the team may identify a great many changes and issues they would like to tackle. But when it comes to process improvement, it is best to introduce only one to two changes every sprint. This makes it easier for the team to judge the relative effect of each change on the overall process.

If the team is able to identify only problems that involve changing others' behaviors but not their own, some coaching is required. Teams that use the retrospective as a forum to complain about everyone else's behavior should be encouraged not just to state problems but also to offer suggestions for improvement. They can even take this a step further by not only describing

---

Agile Tip

While retrospectives may generate lots of problems to be addressed, the team is wise to implement only one to two discrete changes each sprint. Doing so will help them better judge the effectiveness of these changes.

a problem but also including how they personally are going to affect it. For example, a team member may say:

> "Every time we have a user story that requires help from Jane in marketing, we don't get it done by sprint end because she never gets back to us about questions and requirements clarification."

A way to take more accountability in this situation might be by following the above statement with:

> "So from now on, with stories where Jane is involved, I propose we talk to her right at the beginning of the sprint. This will give her more time to respond, and if we are still not hearing from her, we can get our ScrumMaster involved right away."

By including the second statement with the first, the team has moved on from complaining to proposing solutions. They have acknowledged that they can affect the outcome of this situation and have defined the steps to do so.

But the retrospective is also a natural time to identify impediments— problems that truly are outside the realm of the team to solve. Many of these issues are best followed up on by the ScrumMaster outside this meeting. It can be useful for the ScrumMaster to capture these issues in an impediment backlog. This is a prioritized list of issues and problems that the Scrum-Master is working on resolving. In this way, the team can still pick one or two actionable items upon which to act in the next sprint. But they don't lose track of larger issues that are out of their control but, nevertheless, are impacting them dramatically.

Retrospectives are an important part of the Scrum process. As a team is poised between the end of one sprint and the start of the next, it is a natural time to capture their insights and ideas for improvements. Some of the changes implemented through retrospectives are almost minute in nature. But many small changes can add up to huge overall improvements. As with turning the steering wheel of a high-end sports car, many Scrum teams find that tiny adjustments over time are all that are needed to keep them on track and continually improving.

WEEK 3

Week 4 – Estimation, Commitments, and Project Reporting

In Week 4 we'll develop an understanding of how to do long-range planning with Scrum. We'll learn effective estimation techniques and how to create project reports that can be used for tactical and strategic business planning.

Does this sound familiar?

1. Inevitably, in every sprint, we have stories that end up being much larger than the team thought.

2. Planning meetings seem to take forever when the team tries to use relative estimation because they argue about the size of user stories.

3. Our Scrum teams hardly ever meet their sprint commitment.

4. After the team makes a commitment and starts the sprint, the Product Owner adds new work.

5. Our managers don't trust relative estimation so they want us to translate it into hours.

6. Our teams are pushed to increase their velocity—the amount of work they deliver—every sprint.

7. Our director of development has requested personal burndowns for each Scrum team members so she can decide if they are performing well.

8. Management is against Scrum because they say, with Scrum, there is no way to know when a project will be done.

9. Even though each sprint produces a potentially shippable product increment, we still only do releases twice a year

10. We did releases every sprint for a while, but our users complained it was too much work to test new functionality every two weeks.

The purpose of estimation in Scrum differs somewhat from a traditional waterfall project. With a more predictive project-management approach, estimates are gathered from team members so a project manager can make an educated guess as to how long the work will take to complete. Often, with this technique, the emphasis is on the guessing part. The reason for this is simple: having only a high-level knowledge of what is being asked for, team members have very little information on which to base their estimations. As the project starts and new requirements and requests emerge, the true schedule and list of deliverables from the project often drift far away from that original plan.

Agile methods like Scrum know that complex projects require a mechanism with which to regularly gather these new requirements and fold them into the overall plan. Because of this, all agile methods use the concept of iterations. Agile practitioners say, "I know there will be emerging requirements. Because of this, I am going to have pre-planned inspect-and-adapt points in my project. This will give me a built-in way to include this new information in my project plan."

As we've said before, Scrum makes heavy use of the concept of a timebox— a pre-defined amount of time in which a specific goal must be achieved. The typical timebox of a daily Scrum is fifteen minutes. The timebox of a sprint is usually one to four weeks. In both these cases, the varying factor is not time but what can be fit into the time available. In some ways, it is the exact opposite of traditional project management. With waterfall, we said, "This is what I want. How long will it take to build?" In Scrum, we often say the exact opposite: "This is how much time I have. How much can I get in that time?"

The basis of all working product in Scrum is the sprint. Every sprint must produce a potentially shippable product increment. Because of this, estimation techniques used in Scrum focus on tools that help a team increase the likelihood they will make a sprint commitment they can meet. One very popular approach to determining the size of user stories is relative estimation.

The term "relative estimation" has, as its root, the word "relate." Teams that use relative estimation do not try to determine, in an absolute sense, the size of backlog items. Rather, they try to understand the size of a given item in relation to the other items they are considering.

As it turns out, relative estimation mimics nature. Humans are constantly interpreting their world through comparisons and make inferences about similarities and differences. For example, suppose you were asked to estimate the weight, in ounces, of the following items:

- A paper clip
- A deck of cards
- A toaster
- A sledgehammer

To do this exercise, you would visualize the items in your mind, review what knowledge you had about them and make your best guess as to their weights. Now suppose I gave you the same list but a different directive. Suppose this time I asked you to rank those items from heaviest to lightest. How would your thought process differ?

You would still compare the items. But the difference is the whole process of coming to a list ranked heaviest to lightest would take you no more than a couple seconds to construct. This is because you would be using relative estimation to accomplish the task. Rather than getting hung up on how many pounds a typical sledgehammer weighs and how to convert that to ounces, your first thought might be, "Well, the heaviest thing on that list is definitely the sledgehammer." And your mind might seek out the other extreme as well: "The lightest thing on the list has to be the paper clip." To rank the remaining items, you would compare them to each other and to these two extremes: "The deck of cards surely weighs more than the paper clip. And I am pretty sure the toaster would weigh more than the cards but less than the sledgehammer." But because this comparison ranking happens so quickly in your mind, you are almost unaware you are doing it.

This is the process teams use when they do relative estimation. Rather than focusing on how long it will take to complete each user story, they focus instead on trying to understand how many user stories will fit into a given sprint. And a good way to do this is to understand the relative size of each story in comparison to the others being considered. Rather than laboriously generating estimates for work far in advance, only to have them be wrong, teams use a simple, unit-less scale to indicate one story is much more work than another.

WEEK 4

Some teams make up their own relative estimation scales, and others use established patterns, such as the Fibonacci scale. But certainly one of the most popular relative estimation scales is that of T-shirt sizes. When teams use this scale, they designate all of their user stories as either extra-small (XS), small (S), medium (M), large (L), or extra-large (XL). Having a scale with a limited number of choices is like having that few buckets in which to place user stories.

Since, with this scale, there are only five buckets from which to choose, discussions about sizing tend to take less time. To make the process even more effective, teams may use tools like planning poker. With this approach, the team has a special deck of cards that gives each member one card for each of the T-shirt sizes. After a team has discussed a particular PBI and they are ready to estimate its size, they do so by each putting the card in front of them, face down, that they think best represents the size of the story. Then they all turn over their cards at once. Having all cards revealed at once helps ensure all team members give their honest thoughts about the story size without being unduly influenced by their colleagues.

Once sizes are revealed, team members discuss any wide discrepancies. This discussion is very useful because it can serve to point out assumptions and additional information that not all team members may have understood yet. Then the teams re-size using their cards, or they can simply verbally agree to a given size after the discussion.

This ability of relative estimation to reveal hidden information that not every team member may be considering is part of its power. A team member may discover the reason he thought a PBI was "small" and his teammate thought it was "extra-large" was the fact he was forgetting a large portion of the work to be done. Relative estimation can point out these assumptions before the team makes commitments.

Relative estimation is very popular among all agile teams, not just those that do Scrum. But regardless of whether teams use this approach to estimate or do a more traditional, hours-based estimation there are always things that can go wrong. Below are some common problems with the estimation process.

The Foot Draggers

The Problem

One of the great advantages of relative estimation is that it is time-efficient. If you only have five choices, deciding which bucket a given PBI goes into can usually happen in short order after a team discusses the finer points of the requirement. Indeed, the theory behind relative estimation says we can't really know how much work a given user story will require until we start working on it, so getting close is good enough.

> ### Agile Tip
>
> It is important to remember that relative estimation scales are unit-less. That means, if your team uses the Fibonacci scale and sizes a user story as an eight, that does not mean eight hours or eight days. It just means "eight," which is more than five and less than thirteen.

After teams get a little practice with relative estimation, they should find they can do it fairly quickly. So when that shift does not happen, there is reason for concern. Sometimes, even months after they've gotten started with relative estimation, teams still find their estimation takes a long time. Their sprint-planning meetings do not get shorter in length and, indeed, are often a painful process of excruciatingly detailed questions for the Product Owner. The team feels they must know everything before they can estimate, even in a relative fashion. Consequently, they drag their feet about coming to an actual estimate for each story. The resulting effect is sizing takes as long, if not longer, than it did with a more traditional hours-estimation technique.

Why This Happens

The first time or two a team does any kind of relative estimation, it is natural they will fumble a bit over what constitutes, for example, a medium user story. But as they see that estimation is only a means to an end, with the end being a sprint commitment they can likely deliver, they worry less about the actual story sizes and more about making certain they feel comfortable with the sprint commitment as a whole. So when this doesn't happen within a sprint or two, it usually means the team has not made the true mental shift to relative estimation. In their minds, they may be trying to turn their relative scale back into an absolute one.

WEEK 4

With this type of thinking, they may actually be using an estimation process that is essentially the worst of both worlds. In their minds, they estimate in hours and then try to convert that number into a relative estimation size. Needless to say, there are major problems with this approach. Aside from being time-consuming, estimating this way usually means the team member is thinking primarily of his own work. For example, if he is a software developer, he may be thinking only of the time required to write the code for a given user story. But a relative estimate like a T-shirt size represents the total amount of work required to deliver a finished user story. This may need to include the work of testers, user-interface designers, technical writers, and more. If the entire team is still thinking in this absolute estimation fashion, where they run into real trouble is when they try to put these estimates together to agree on a single size for a user story. Particularly when a PBI is work-intensive for only one role (for example, the development is easy, but the testing effort is very hard), it can be difficult for teams to come to consensus if they have not truly embraced relative estimation. Conversation tends to get bogged down, and team members are reluctant to agree to a size, much to the frustration of the Product Owner and ScrumMaster.

The Fix

One of the most challenging things about helping a team that is clinging to absolute-estimation thinking is that they often don't realize they are doing so. In their minds, you asked them to come up with a T-shirt size that represents the effort in the PBI, and that is what they are trying to do. But they are going about it in an unnecessarily laborious way.

Getting a team to make the true mental shift to relative estimation, as opposed to just going through the motions, is tricky. For such teams, it is often good for the ScrumMaster to take a more active facilitation role during sizing. When a user story has disproportionate work, meaning one or more team members will need to put forth much more effort than the others, the ScrumMaster can simply say something to this effect: "Ok, so it sounds as if the testing effort is really large for this PBI, whereas the development effort is quite small, so keep that in mind when you are ready to size this story." The team's discussion around estimation can often spin, meaning team members get caught up in details and lose sight of the overall goal. By simply summarizing and restating a ten-minute conversation about a given PBI, the ScrumMaster can bring organization to the discussion and help the team move forward.

A structured approach like planning poker works well for teams that are still struggling to embrace the concept of relative estimation. Taking this structure a step further can also be helpful. Many teams have standard rules for how to estimate when team members disagree. One such rule is, "When in doubt, round up." In other words, if the debate is between whether a user story is a small or a medium, default to medium. Another example of a standardized rule is, "If we disagree, we vote, and majority rules." In both these cases, it is important to have the rule in place and agreed upon before it is used. The ScrumMaster can propose this idea, for example, in the retrospective. If the team is open to the idea, they can define the rule ahead of time and then use it when needed.

If teams still struggle with relative estimation months after learning the technique, some shock therapy may be in order. When coaching such teams, I want them to understand that estimation is only a means to an end—the sprint commitment is that end. So when teams continually struggle with the concepts, I request they make commitments for their next sprint doing no estimation whatsoever. "That is impossible!" they say. "We have to know how big a user story is before we can commit to it!" But that belief is not entirely accurate. It is true the team needs to have a general sense of the work involved in delivering a backlog item before they can make a commitment. But often their gut feeling about how much work this constitutes is a much better gauge of effort that a laborious estimate in hours. When a team makes a sprint commitment with no estimation, they will often stop using estimates as a crutch and think in a more holistic sense about the user story and its size. Indeed, some advanced Scrum teams do not estimate at all—they simply make sprint commitments. These teams have truly internalized the purpose of estimation. It is simply a means to an end. And when such team members make statements like, "I can't put my finger on it but I have a feeling this user story is more complicated than in looks on the surface," ScrumMasters and Product Owners are wise to listen and support this hunch.

WEEK 4

The Ego War

The Problem

A team goes through a multi-layered thought and discussion process to come to agreement on a relative estimation size for a PBI. First they may think only of their own tasks required for the estimate. But next, they want to hear from their teammates about what other work might be needed. Finally, the team tries to think of anything else that might impact the size of the user story. All these factors are considered when deciding on a final size for the PBI.

Not surprisingly, with impact factors emerging at different layers, teams can get bogged down in their effort to come to consensus on the size of a story. Sometimes, particularly when a team is still learning to work together in an agile way, these discussions can become less about agreeing to a reasonable size for a story and more about being right. In such cases, team members dig in and argue for their particular belief. No longer focused on coming to consensus, team members want to win by persuading everyone else over to their way of thinking. Such Ego Wars can drag down an estimation session. Teams may literally spend an hour arguing over whether a user story is a medium or a large. When this happens, as with the Foot Draggers, estimating takes much longer than it should, and the benefits of relative estimation disappear.

Why This Happens

Ego wars can happen when the Scrum team is a group of strong individuals. Particularly when they are senior technical people used to acting in a leading role, they are used to making decisions on the behalf of others. In many non-agile organizations, technical leads are responsible for generating estimates for the entire team. Being used to this authoritative role, it can take a while for them to remember how to come to consensus and listen to others' opinions.

Then, too, the Scrum team itself may still be in its "storming" phase. While still learning to work together, these conflicts are normal. Team members are jockeying for their place in the group. Something simple, like winning an argument about the size of a user story, takes on an outsized meaning. It can make a team member feel she is appreciated and respected within the group.

The Fix

Teams that struggle with ego battles during estimation get less benefit from tools like planning poker. Instead, with these teams, the ScrumMaster should consider using active facilitation for estimation sessions. One of the best things to do is to get a "stake in the ground," meaning trying to establish the smallest and biggest user stories. This can be done by presenting a group of PBIs and simply asking, "Of the stories we are considering, does anyone have a strong feeling about which one is one of the smallest?" Note we say "one of the smallest" not "the smallest." Staying away from absolutes will help keep people from getting entrenched in their opinions. Do the same for some of the largest user stories. Then simply start comparing those in the middle. But do this in a way that keeps the language neutral. Rather than saying, "Is Story B a medium or a large?" compare it to a story whose size has already been established: "We said Story A was a small. Is Story B bigger than that?" If the team says yes, the ScrumMaster can follow up with, "Is it a little bigger (a medium) or a lot bigger (a large)?" Simply keeping this neutral language during sizing can do a great deal to lower the tensions of an estimation session and remind teams that the estimation here truly is relative. With only five PBI sizes from which to choose, it becomes less important if a given story ends up being a medium or large and more important that the team members understand what goes into delivering the story—the acceptance criteria and tasks. A good rule of thumb for teams and ScrumMasters is this: if, after establishing the acceptance criteria and tasks for a given story, you've argued more than ten minutes about its size, just flip a coin. That assessment is fast and is as likely to give an accurate estimate as another half-hour of arguing.

The Iceberg

The Problem

Teams estimate the backlog from the top down. Typically, someone will read the number one user story on the backlog, along with its acceptance criteria. By doing this, the team is getting very clear on what is being asked for. But to get to an estimate, the discussion must move into the "how," meaning how a team intends to fulfill the user story. This discussion includes many elements: how much work might be involved for each team member, outside dependencies, technical complications, and the like. This

WEEK 4

conversation happens for each backlog item that might possibly make it into the sprint commitment.

Sooner or later, every team gets bitten by a user story—something that looked fairly simple to accomplish actually turns out to be much more complicated. But if these unpleasant surprises happen on a regular basis, closer examination is required. Often, in such cases, teams are not delving deeply enough into everything affecting the overall effort of the user story. Particularly when a PBI has dependencies on outside entities, the team may not be thinking of all the work involved in delivering a user story. Like an iceberg, the work required at first glance to complete a user story is not the whole picture. Other issues lurk under the surface, and if the team does not probe to discover those issues, they can be in for unpleasant surprises.

Why This Happens

Teams can find themselves with an Iceberg PBI for a number of reasons. One of the common reasons a user story ends up being much larger than originally thought is that the team did not think through the tasks well. Rather than underestimating given tasks in a PBI, they simply forget to include whole sets of tasks. As we've said before, some advanced teams do not need to estimate in order to make a sprint commitment. But what they do need is to develop a sense of the body of work involved in delivering a PBI. Creating a thorough list of tasks is one way to do this.

Teams may also forget to consider the impact of outsiders on their project. A simple task to generate test data may only take a couple hours to achieve. But if selecting the correct data requires meeting with a particular stakeholder whose schedule is extremely busy, the work may actually take much longer. When teams forget to take into account these outside influences when they size a story, they can be negatively surprised when the work takes much longer to complete that they thought.

The Fix

The key to understanding the true size of a user story is not in the magic of any particular estimation technique. It is more about doing a thorough job of describing and considering the work involved to deliver a PBI. And "work" is about more than just writing and testing code. Taking the time to develop a comprehensive task list for each user story is the first step in avoiding Iceberg PBIs. But beyond the hours they themselves will put into a user story, the team should also talk about what outside impacts might affect their ability to deliver on their commitments. For example, maybe a stakeholder has developed a reputation with the team as being slow to work with. Any assistance or feedback required from that person seems to take twice as long to get as it should. It is perfectly reasonable that teams bump up the estimate of a given user story to reflect that. When teams estimate a user story, they must think of everything that goes into creating the final deliverable. If there are outside forces that the team believes make that harder to do, that should be reflected in their estimate.

> **Agile Tip**
>
> Sooner or later, every team gets surprised by a user story that was much bigger than they originally thought. Encourage teams to use the retrospective meeting to talk about why this happened and if there would be a way to prevent similar surprises in the future.

Any organization moving to an agile way of thinking must always keep firmly in mind that estimation is nothing more than a means to an end. Even with traditional project management methods, this is true. Estimates are simply a way for project managers to predict when the project might be done. Agile methods like Scrum realized the folly of taking estimates that might be made months before a line of code was written and treating them like law. Instead, good agile teams know how much their organizations value them delivering what they said they would in a sprint. Using a technique like relative estimation is one way to help them increase the odds of doing this. It gives them a quick and efficient way to be able to say, "This PBI is going to be much more work that the other one." And they can use this information to make a sprint commitment with confidence, which is, of course, the whole point.

Sprint Commitment—The Scrum Team's Perspective

A Scrum team is well aware that their Product Owner comes into a sprint-planning meeting looking to get from them a sprint commitment. So their concern is to get enough information about each user story to make an educated

WEEK 4

guess as to whether or not it will fit into the upcoming sprint. As we've seen, estimating user stories is one tool teams uses to help make that judgment.

Once user stories are estimated, teams turn to another agile concept to help them decide how much can fit into a sprint: yesterday's weather. This term comes from the old adage, "Given no other information, the best predictor of today's weather is yesterday's weather." Likewise, Scrum teams know that, given no other information, the best predictor of what they can deliver in the upcoming sprint is the amount of work they delivered in the last sprint.

To measure the total amount of work done in a sprint, teams use the idea of story points. Story points give a relative weight to each user story size. Very large PBIs are worth more story points than small ones. Teams can use any consistent story-point scale they like. When teams estimate using the Fibonacci scale, the numbers themselves become the story points. For example, let's stay a team uses this portion of the Fibonacci scale for estimation: 1, 2, 3, 5, 8, 13. Let's also say last sprint they were able to commit to and deliver the following:

> **Agile Tip**
>
> The ultimate goal of estimation is to help the team make a sprint commitment they can likely meet. It must be kept firmly in mind that estimation is only a means to this end.

Relative Size on Fibonacci Scale	User Stories in the Sprint of That Size	Total Story-point Count for That User Story Size
1	4	4
2	3	6
3	1	3
5	0	0
8	2	16
13	0	0
Total Story Points in Sprint:		29

In our example above, you can simply add the numbers in the far right column to see that this team had a total sprint commitment of twenty-nine story points. So in their next sprint-planning meeting, they can use that as a guide. There total commitment should be a set of user stories whose estimates total to around twenty-nine story points.

When teams use a non-numerical scale for estimation, like T-shirt sizes, they need only add on a numeric weighting to use the same technique. Using a "powers of two" scale is common, as follows:

XS = 1 story point
S   = 2 story points
M   = 4 story points
L   = 8 story points
XL = 16 story points

With such a scale, this team can use yesterday's weather as well. If, in the last sprint, they delivered four small user stories, three mediums, and two larges, we would say they delivered a total of thiry-six story points. The story point metric is a powerful tool for both short- and long-term planning. Over time, the number of story points a team delivers tends to normalize, meaning it is about the same from sprint to sprint. This helps them have more confidence in their sprint commitments. It also helps the Product Owner with long-term planning. The average number of story points a team can deliver each sprint is known as their velocity. Once a Product Owner knows his team's velocity and he also knows how many total story points are in a given release, he can start to make some very good educated guesses as to how many sprints will be required to complete the whole release. Best of all, he can make these predictions based not on made-up estimates done months before but real data about how the team is performing.

So, as we've seen, commitments are an important part of making Scrum projects more predictable. But, like everything else, problems can occur in the commitment process. Because a sprint commitment is the product of the Scrum team/Product Owner relationship, problems with commitment can originate with either side. Let's look at sprint commitment issues that come from the team members.

Agile Tip

Story points are a weighted numeric value given to relative estimation scales. They are useful in determining a team's velocity— the amount of work they can produce from sprint to sprint.

WEEK 4

The Eternal Optimists

The Problem

Once a team has established a regular velocity, the actual process to make a sprint commitment becomes quite mechanical. If, for example, a team has a historical velocity of about thirty story points per sprint, they can simply go down the backlog, accepting user stories into the sprint, until the total story points are close to thirty. At that point, the sprint is full, and no further commitments are made.

Sometimes the cut-off point between stories is not so neat. For example, a team may be at twenty-eight story points for commitment, but the next story in line is eight story points, which would put them over their historical velocity. At that point, the team must make a judgment call. Should they take on the extra story, knowing it is a little ambitious, or not? It truly is up to them. It is perfectly OK for teams to take on an ambitious commitment in a sprint, provided they have a plan for how to deliver.

Unfortunately, some Scrum teams are long on the ambitious part of their commitment but decidedly short on having an actual plan to deliver the PBIs to which they committed. Ever the Eternal Optimists. If they miss a sprint commitment, they insist that was because of extenuating circumstances. "That was due to a production problem that comes up once in a blue moon!" they say. Maybe so. But when a team continually takes on more than they can deliver in a sprint, problems occur. That wonderful predictability that makes Product Owners' lives easier disappears as the amount of work a team commits to in a sprint often bears little if any relation to what they actually deliver.

Why This Happens

There are many reasons why a team may perpetually overcommit. One reason may be a reluctance to admit they are taking on more work than they can reasonably deliver. Scrum teams take pride in their ability to deliver value to the business. It can be hard for them to admit that even they have limits. Hearing excuses like, "We missed our commitment because of this unusual event that happened," bear a closer look. Maybe this is true. But if these "unusual events" crop up five sprints in a row, it is time to accept that the sprint commitment needs to be adjusted to reflect this.

A common time this will happen is when a team puts their product into production for the first time. If they are now responsible for both production support and developing new enhancements, they will find the amount of time they have available for the new work has dropped. The difference between what they used to be able to deliver in a sprint and what they can now deliver is reflected in the time they spend supporting their product. This change must be reflected in future sprint commitments.

Teams also overcommit when they have not fully internalized what "sprint commitment" means. They might view it as something much more casual and will say things like, "Sure, we will give it a try." Maybe they feel pressure to say yes to absolutely everything the Product Owner requests. Or maybe they simply don't understand what a difficult position the Product Owner will be in when he tells stakeholders they are going to receive given features in a sprint and they don't get completed. In any of these cases, the real problem is that there is no penalty to the team for missing a sprint commitment. If stakeholders are angry or the release is delayed, that's the Product Owner's problem. They simply continue on, protected by the ScrumMaster and, in this case, especially by the Product Owner, never having to answer for why they did not deliver what they said they would.

The Fix

Regardless of the reason a team might perpetually overcommit, the first step in fixing the problem is always the same. Teams should use yesterday's weather to make sprint commitments. If history shows they can deliver thirty story points a sprint, then commitments of forty, fifty, or sixty story points should not even be considered. Teams often feel outside pressure to commit to more each sprint. Using yesterday's weather as evidence can be a powerful argument to even non-Scrum stakeholders as to why this is a bad idea. The ScrumMaster should strongly encourage a team to keep their commitments within what yesterday's weather says is reasonable.

Using yesterday's weather to make commitments should fix the problem of overcommitting. But the ScrumMaster should give some thought as to why the team fell into perpetually overcommitting in the first place. Do they feel pressured by the Product Owner to constantly take on more? Or do they not take the idea of commitment seriously? In any case, understanding why

WEEK 4

teams overcommit in the first place can help a ScrumMaster know where she can provide coaching in the future to make certain teams do not fall into this habit again.

The Perpetual Pessimists

The Problem

At the other extreme, far from their glass-half-full counterparts, are the perpetual pessimists. The pessimists always want to undercommit. Even if history shows their team can deliver thirty story points in a sprint, they are reluctant to commit to that amount. A commitment of twenty-five seems safer, they will argue. Their attitude is, "It is always better to under-promise and over-deliver." To give evidence that this approach is the right one, they may cite times when outside influences interfered with their ability to deliver on commitments. In their minds, these and other unplanned events are good arguments for holding out some capacity for unplanned work.

Why This Happens

An important thing to note with pessimists is that often this behavior is the perfectly logical output of what the team has been told or what they have intuited. Sometimes Product Owners inadvertently encourage a team to make commitments this way by implying disaster will strike if the sprint commitment is missed. Consider this statement by a Product Owner: "You guys absolutely cannot miss the sprint commitment because the clients are asking to know ahead of time what they will be seeing in the sprint review." Needless to say, when such a dire statement is made to a team, Product Owners should not be surprised that the team commits conservatively.

> ## Agile Tip
>
> Teams should rely on yesterday's weather—the amount of work they have delivered in past sprints—to indicate the amount of work they should commit to in future sprints.

An even more insidious problem is when teams seem literally frightened at the prospect of missing a sprint commitment. This can be a red flag, warning of serious problems. Organizations that produce pessimistic teams often have a culture of fear. In these enterprises, making mistakes is not tolerated. As a consequence, employees are far more concerned with not being wrong than with being right. This means they will take a tried-and-true solution that produces mediocre results over a riskier approach that might yield greater benefits. Organizations that have a culture of fear are notorious for having teams that not only undercommit but also balk at making any commitments at all.

The Fix

If a Product Owner has been sending the team an unintentional message about commitments that encourages undercommitting, that is relatively easy to remedy. Once aware of his behavior, the Product Owner can decide if this very conservative approach is what he really wants. If it is not, then he needs to adjust his message to the team. So in the example above, the Product Owner can tweak his message slightly to sound less dire: "The clients have asked me to let them know ahead of time what features we will demo in the sprint review. I'd like to get your thoughts on what I should tell them." With this approach, the Product Owner works with the team to set stakeholder expectations for the sprint. He is acknowledging that a sprint commitment is not a promise written in blood but a promise given in good faith. Taking this approach puts the Product Owner and team on the same side, which is important for their long-term relationship.

The "culture of fear" problem is much more difficult to fix, in part, because organizations are reluctant to admit or acknowledge that they do this. Often, managers in such enterprises will talk about valuing innovation and taking chances. These statements may even be on a plaque somewhere in the office, espoused as organizational values. But people believe what they see in action, not what they are told. The risk in a willingness to take chances is that sometimes the chances don't work out. If that possibility is not accepted, then an organization does not truly value risk-taking.

Agile teams have a saying: "We like to fail fast." This means they understand that discovering the right path means trying and subsequently eliminating some paths that are not going to work out. Good teams would rather try those "wrong" paths and toss them from the possible

> **Agile Tip**
>
> When teams are told they must meet their sprint commitment "no matter what," they often respond by being very conservative in their commitment. This is a natural and very rational response to being told that missing a commitment will have grave consequences.

WEEK 4

solution sooner rather than later. Think of it this way: if you are a university student and you have chosen the wrong major, would you rather know this two semesters into your degree program or one semester before you graduate? In organizations that give only lip service to risk-taking, the ScrumMaster has some work to do. She must begin a dialogue with organizational leaders that gently but firmly helps them realize they have been sending mixed messages. Changes in a business culture do not happen overnight. But even having the Scrum inner circle—the ScrumMaster, Product Owner, and Scrum team—see and acknowledge this problem can be an important first step in bringing this issue to light in the whole organization.

The Cherry Pickers

The Problem

The balance of power and responsibility in Scrum is set up to ultimately benefit most the project itself. For example, the Product Owner has final say on the order of the product backlog itself. But the team has final say on how many of those items will be moved into Sprint commitment. The result of this division of responsibility is the organization always gets as much high value functionality as possible each sprint.

But when the Scrum roles become blurred, the value of the sprint output can be impaired. Such is the case when teams do not make commitments from the backlog in top-down order but, rather, choose what they will work on. Cherry Pickers take from the backlog the things they would like to work on, rather than those items the Product Owner has designated as most important. As a result, the organization is no longer guaranteed it will receive the highest-value backlog items first. Instead, it gets what the team feels like committing to and building.

Why This Happens

Several reasons explain why teams revert to cherry-picking behavior. Teams that are used to working in a more waterfall approach are often accustomed to long development times, often of many months. With this approach, the stakeholders don't see the working product until the end. So it is natural that the teams organize the work according to what is most convenient for them.

It can take some rethinking for these teams to shift to delivering first what the organization most needs to see.

A team may also use cherry-picking behavior to subtly bully a Product Owner. If the backlog is ordered in a way that is inconvenient for them, they simply choose a different set of backlog items, insisting the work must be done in that order. In such cases, the Product Owner may wonder why he even prioritizes the backlog at all since the team chooses what they will work on from all potential PBIs. He is right to wonder this—there is no point putting together an ordered product backlog if, in the end, the team simply ignores that ordering.

But occasionally cherry-picking behavior can arise from a team honestly trying to do the right thing. Sometimes the order of user stories in the backlog will be such that a team does not quite fill its sprint commitment based on yesterday's weather. But adding the next item on the list puts the sprint commitment well over the limit. This can particularly be a problem when the Product Owner has several very large PBIs sitting right at the top of the backlog. Often, only one or two of these will fit into a sprint commitment. So the team then looks through the backlog, trying to select smaller PBIs that will fill in the gap and make a complete sprint commitment.

A similar thing can happen when a team realizes it would be advantageous to do two or more backlog items at the same time. Often, non-technical Product Owners do not understand which backlog items are related to each other in a technical way. This is not always obvious from the business requirements themselves. But Scrum teams, with their technical expertise, do know this. They may cherry-pick the backlog in an effort to consolidate work and limit the times they touch a given piece of code.

The Fix

Teams should accept, as a default, the Product Owner's ordering of the backlog. It is his responsibility to determine which backlog items are most valued by the organization and see those delivered first. However, a good Product Owner knows that prioritization by business value is only the first step in ordering his product backlog. Nearly as important is how much effort it will take to build a PBI. This is the basic cost-benefit equation by which Product Owners judge all items on their backlog. The business value is the

WEEK 4

benefit, but the effort required to build a PBI is the cost. A shrewd Product Owner is always combing his backlog, looking for items which will bring lots of benefit but at very little cost.

One way to do this is to order the backlog with a two-part process. First, based on business value alone, the Product Owner can do an initial prioritization of the backlog. But then he may ask the team about sizing. He may also ask their advice about moving certain backlog items around to make actual development of the product easier. With all these actions, the Product Owner is trying to tease out more value from the backlog.

This kind of negotiation between the team and Product Owner is fine and indeed a very good thing to do—but not in sprint planning. As we've said before, having a smooth sprint-planning meeting requires the Product Owner coming in with a backlog that is already in order. A better place for juggling backlog items and experimenting with what-if scenarios is the backlog-grooming session. This meeting is the perfect venue for the team and Product Owner to work together to put the backlog in an order that gives very high value to the organization. Ultimately, the Product Owner still has final say on the order. But he gets valuable advice and input from the team to reach that decision.

Sprint Commitment—The Product Owner's and Stakeholders' Perspectives

In the last section, we looked at what can go wrong during the sprint commitment process from the team's perspective. But sprint commitment is really a two-way street. The commitment is the team's promise to the Product Owner to make a good faith effort to deliver those items within the sprint. But the Product Owner also has a commitment to the team. Once the sprint has started, the work statement becomes locked down. No further work is added. If a Product Owner comes to a team three days into a two-week sprint and says, "Hey, that item I told you was number one on the backlog—I changed my mind about it. I don't want it anymore," he is not holding up his part of the bargain.

A good Product Owner is always looking to get more value out of a sprint. But sometimes, in a desire to achieve more, he can overstep the bounds of his role and start to impair the team's ability to work effectively. Stakeholders can do this as well. Below are some of the negative behaviors you may see from Product Owners and stakeholders that could affect the sprint commitment process.

The Magic Box

The Problem

One of the key benefits of Scrum is that teams get the length of a sprint to work essentially uninterrupted. Creative technical work requires mental focus. Before Scrum, teams may have found themselves responding on an hour-by-hour basis to requests and issues. Spending their days in such a reactive way is both unpleasant and ineffective. But working within the boundaries of a sprint, the decision about what to focus on is made up front. Once the sprint starts, the team knows they will be free to organize their time as they wish, protected from outside interference by the ScrumMaster and Product Owner.

But sometimes, this wall of protection is not as solid as it should be. A Product Owner may come to the team mid-sprint with additions or changes to the backlog. Sometimes this new work is unavoidable. If a team is responsible for production support of a system and a major problem occurs, no doubt, they will need to drop everything and fix the issue. But sometimes the emergency is not such an emergency at all. A powerful stakeholder may suddenly decide he has to have a PBI in a given sprint. Or the Product Owner may simply change his mind about what he wants in the sprint. Regardless of the source, changes to the sprint are always disruptive to the team. But they are particularly problematic when there is no adjustment to the original commitment of the sprint. Yesterday's weather tells us about how much work can fit into a sprint. A sprint is like a box that holds, for example, about thirty story points worth of work. So if new items come into the sprint, something else must come out to make room. The size of the box cannot change. Problems occur when a Product Owner will not accept this fact. In his mind, the sprint is a Magic Box. Like a magician, he wants to be able to stuff more and more into the sprint and somehow have it all magically get done.

WEEK 4

Why This Happens

As we've said, Product Owners are often pressured by the organization to constantly deliver more value. In his reluctance to disappoint certain key stakeholders, a Product Owner may lack the fortitude to push back on requests that come in mid-sprint. He may plead with the team to try to fit the extra work in "just this once." But he is setting a dangerous habit and ignoring the laws of physics as well. If a team has used yesterday's weather to make a sprint commitment, then the sprint is already full. Adding in a new requirement means something else must come out. Pretending this is not so will ultimately serve no one in the end.

Even in the case of production support issues, what constitutes an emergency bears close scrutiny. Not every production problem needs to be fixed immediately. Sometimes, just adding the fix to the backlog of the next sprint is the right solution. If a Product Owner's immediate reaction to all production problems is, "Drop everything and fix this right now," he may simply be overlooking the fact that there could be other options.

The Fix

The first step in fixing the Magic Box problem is getting everyone to understand and accept that there is no such thing as a Magic Box. After a Scrum team has established a regular velocity, the amount of work that will fit into a sprint is known. Simply wishing this number was bigger won't change it. So a ground rule should be, "If something new absolutely must come into the sprint, an equivalent amount of work from the original sprint commitment must be removed." And it is the Product Owner's job to choose what work now will not get done. These are often very difficult tradeoffs, but they must be made. It ultimately does not serve the Product Owner, the team, or even the stakeholders to pretend this isn't true.

> **Agile Tip**
>
> The amount of work deliverable in a sprint is constant. If the Product Owner must add new items to the sprint after commitment has been made, then he must also choose which items from the original commitment will now be taken out.

Teams that do production support may choose to track about how much effort they typically put into that work. If it is somewhat consistent over time, they may argue to withhold some of their capacity from the total sprint commitment in anticipation of these fixes and requests. Some teams even have a backlog item they include in each sprint called "production issues." Teams that do this feel it is important to have this work represented on the backlog so Product Owners and stakeholders can see how much of their time it is taking.

But any time new work comes up mid-sprint, it is always worth asking, "Why did we not know about this before the sprint started?" True, sometimes emergencies come up, and there is no way to anticipate them. But when new, high-priority PBIs continually crop up after the sprint has started, it may mean the Product Owner is not giving enough attention to backlog prioritization. If he knows he can make changes after a sprint starts, a Product Owner may get a bit lazy about making certain the order of his backlog truly represents his top priorities. This should be discussed in the retrospective. As the saying goes: "A failure to plan on your part does not constitute an emergency on my part." It is not unreasonable for the Scrum team to feel this way. They should work closely with the Product Owner to keep these mid-sprint surprises to a minimum.

Lost in Translation

The Problem

Though Scrum teams often adapt very easily to the concept of story points, the rest of the organization can have a harder time. Managers may feel uncomfortable with this new way of judging what will fit into a sprint. "So what constitutes a 'medium' user story anyway?" they may ask. They still see their role as supervisory—they are there to make sure people get work done. The desire to check up on the self-managing Scrum team can be overwhelming.

Many teams that size user stories via relative estimation do not bother to estimate the tasks themselves. They feel if they understand the total body of work that goes into fulfilling a user story (the acceptance criteria and tasks) and have an overall feel for its size, this is enough to help them decide if they can include the story in a sprint. For organizations whose managers fill their days monitoring people to determine if they are using their time well, this change is often too much for them to take.

So they come up with a suggestion. They would like to create a "translation scale" that equates the story-point scale with hours or days. They may say, "Let's say any story that takes a day or less is an XS. A story that takes two to three days is an S." And so on. Organizations that use the Fibonacci scale seem particularly vulnerable to falling into this trap, because the scale is only numeric. It can be very tempting to say a story that is an eight on the Fibonacci scale is will take eight days to complete.

The problem with this approach is two-fold. First, it gets teams back into the business of counting up hours and not looking at the story holistically. We've discussed the problems this can cause. Team members tend to think only about their own work, and they do not tend to have as thorough group discussions as when the whole group must come to a consensus on a size. Second and far worse is the message this sends the team. When managers want to translate relative estimation into hours, it is clear they don't trust the team to manage their time well. Team members can read between the lines. Using our example above, if they size a story as an XS and it ends up taking three days to complete, they are in trouble with management, despite the fact they may have met their sprint commitment just fine.

Why This Happens

When managers push teams to translate story points into hours, they are sending a clear message of lack of trust. Such organizations often have a rather old-fashioned, "theory X" view of the role of managers. They see them as the individuals charged with telling people what to do and then monitoring their work to make certain they do it. People who subscribe to these management beliefs are genuinely baffled as to how an agile approach could ever work. "How do I know the team will do anything they've committed to if I don't closely monitor them throughout the sprint?" they may ask.

Of course, the problem is that they are missing the whole point of the self-managed team. What matters is that a team meets its sprint commitment. That is what will produce predictability—a regular velocity—over time and make it much easier to do business planning. In the long run, a small user story that turned out to be more like a medium doesn't really matter. It is up to the team to take responsibility for figuring out how to meet the sprint commitment, despite these surprises.

And they are not likely to take on that responsibility if they feel they are being treated like children, always being made to justify how they are spending their time. Over-monitoring by managers tends to inhibit self-management. In such an accusatory environment, the team no longer works as a unit but often will revert to defensive behaviors. Made constantly to justify how they use their time, they will probably start to pad estimates, just to avoid confrontation. And because they will be criticized if a medium story doesn't take the appropriate number of days to complete that it should, they will make certain the numbers add up on paper, even if in reality their time was spent differently. At its worst, when managers excessively monitor how agile teams use their time, the team simply tells management what it wants to hear. They say what they need to say, regardless of whether it matches reality, to make management happy so they can be left alone to work in peace.

The Fix

It is almost impossible to get dramatic benefits from Scrum if the only changes that occur take place in the individuals that make up the Scrum inner circle. Teams can try to self-manage, but if their own managers oppose this effort, there is only so much a team can do. A more wide-scale culture change is necessary, and it must start with organization management.

Managers must learn that, with Scrum and other agile methods, their role in the organization has now changed. Instead of being charged with monitoring work, their primary role now is to remove impediments. As we've said, a ScrumMaster will identify and (with the help of the team) prioritize impediments. But they will usually need management to help remove these problems because managers have the budget and authority to do so.

This shift can be wonderfully liberating for managers who embrace this idea. It gets them out of the business of babysitting. Instead, they can treat team members like the intelligent, responsible people they are. They learn that what matters is the sprint commitment, not the hours spent on any given user story. Because of the time-boxed nature of Scrum, the total number of hours available is known. So the question then becomes, "How do we use those hours most effectively to deliver what we said we would deliver?" Managers will add far more value in an agile organization by removing impediments that interfere with a team's ability to deliver than they ever will by demanding explanations for why a particular PBI took two extra days to complete.

WEEK 4

When they realize this and their actions reflect this realization, the team will respond by taking ownership of their own work.

The Pressure Cooker

The Problem

Once a Product Owner learns the value of the velocity metric, he will often enthusiastically embrace it as an aid in long-term planning. Rather than relying on projections, which are essentially guesses about how much work a team can do, he can use historical data and establish trends. If he knows how many story points a team can produce each sprint and how many story points are in the entire release, then his ability to predict when the release will be done is quite good.

Velocity is a tantalizing metric. Unfortunately, the temptation to try to manipulate velocity sometimes proves too much for Product Owners and stakeholders. They may look at a team's velocity and wonder, "Could they produce more?" They may pressure a team to commit to and deliver more each sprint, thinking that an increase in the team's velocity is proof they are becoming more efficient. This is especially likely to happen when commitments have been made up front to customers. Often teams are told, "We have to deliver the product in twelve weeks. Figure out how to do it." Scrum teams may even be pitted against one another. "Team A produces forty story points a sprint, and you guys only produce thirty. Why are you so lazy?"

This kind of interference has a very negative effect on the team. They feel extreme pressure to produce a given result, regardless of whether history shows that result is even possible. Often teams in this kind of pressure-cooker environment will say, "Our management makes promises, and we are supposed to figure some way to deliver on them." Understandably, these teams feel like scapegoats. Their management made bad decisions, and now it is up to them to make it right. At its worst, teams in organizations that use these kinds of pressure tactics may grow to hate Scrum. In their minds and from what they have experienced, Scrum is just a way to work a team more and more each sprint until they are completely used up.

Why This Happens

The pressure-cooker environment can arise from a number of causes. As we've said before, the velocity metric defines the size of the box—how much work a given team can deliver from sprint to sprint. Simply wishing the box is bigger does not make it so. It is true that a team's velocity will often increase over the first few sprints. But this is more about progressing on the learning curve than anything else. For example, the first time a new team tries Scrum, they may commit very conservatively. This is understandable. It is a new process, they are not yet good at it, and they are feeling unsure. It is not unusual for new teams to deliver several extra backlog items in their first sprint as they discover they can actually do more work than they thought.

But a trend will be established fairly quickly. Usually within a few sprints, a team's velocity will stabilize. After that point, any attempt to manipulate the metric will cause compromises in the quality of the sprint's output.

Sometimes managers are fooled into thinking their pressure tactics are working. "I told them they needed to produce an extra twenty story points this sprint or else. And they did it." The problem is this extra work comes at a cost, and the cost is quality. Teams that are forced into producing more than their velocity says they can, immediately start looking for places to cut corners. They take shortcuts. They don't update documentation. They skip parts of testing. All these compromises make a system much harder and more expensive to maintain. This is such a pervasive problem in organizations that agile teams have a name for it: technical debt. Technical debt is weaknesses built into the product due in large part to trying to hit unrealistic schedules.

The problem with technical debt is that it doesn't grow in a linear fashion, but an exponential one. For example, a team member rushes in a piece of code in an effort to meet schedule. It is sloppy and poorly documented, but it works. The next time someone tries to update that functionality, she finds it hard to understand and work with. So she slaps in her fix too, vowing to come back later and clean it up in her spare time. Except that spare time never materializes.

At its worst, technical debt can overwhelm a system, resulting in "technical death." You know you have a system in technical death when teams spend virtually all of their time fixing problems and the velocity of new features creeps down close to zero. Systems laden with technical debt are frustrating

WEEK 4

and time-consuming to work on. Often a simple change in one area of the system will cause a cascade of errors in other, seemingly unrelated, places. Systems mired in technical debt eventually become impractical to maintain. They must either be cleaned up or replaced.

The Fix

Product Owners and stakeholders need to accept that a team's velocity represents reality. Rather than pushing a team continually to achieve more, they should encourage them to work at a sustainable pace. "Sustainable pace" is defined as the velocity at which the team could function effectively forever. No one can scramble madly all the time. The predictability of a Scrum team's output will dramatically increase when the idea of sustainable pace is supported by the organization.

> ### Agile Tip
>
> The goal of Scrum is for teams to work at a sustainable, not ever-increasing, pace.

Product Owners and ScrumMasters can support a team's right to work at a sustainable pace. Managing stakeholders' expectations may be necessary. Product Owners in particular must always remember the "iron triangle," meaning the tradeoffs between cost, features, and schedule. Since most organizations have limited budgets, the true tradeoff is usually between features and schedule. If schedule is fixed ("we must deliver on May 1"), then the number of features included must flex. Likewise, if features are fixed ("we absolutely must have all this functionality"), then schedule must flex. To pretend otherwise is simply not facing reality. Pressuring a team to deliver more might give the illusion that more work is being done. But, in reality, just the opposite is occurring.

Managing the Project—The Sprint

Given that the whole structure of a project changes when Scrum is used, it is natural that the reporting and monitoring of the project should also change. At a basic level, the first place to look to determine the health of a Scrum project is the sprint itself. Indeed, a key purpose of the daily Scrum is to monitor sprint health and for team members to evaluate if they feel on track to meet their sprint commitment.

As we mentioned earlier, a tool many teams find useful to help this effort is the sprint burndown chart, which provides a graphical representation of the amount of work left to do versus the time left to do it in. A sprint burndown chart may be a simple hand-drawn chart on a whiteboard, or it may be electronically generated. But regardless of the level of sophistication, all sprint burndowns give the same information. They help teams, ScrumMasters, and Product Owners judge the likelihood that the sprint commitment will be met.

If a sprint burndown gives clues that the sprint commitment may be in danger, the team has some decisions to make. Perhaps they need to reevaluate how they are approaching the work. Or they may need to raise impediments to their ScrumMaster to get some help. They may even need to renegotiate with their Product Owner what they will be able to deliver in the sprint. In these cases, the sprint burndown acts as an early warning system for the team. It can show them in black-and-white what they may suspect: that the sprint is in danger and actions must be taken.

But sprint burndowns are open to both misinterpretation and manipulation. Sometimes these problems arise when stakeholders view the burndown. They often misinterpret the chart's data and what conclusions they can draw from that information. But even within the Scrum inner circle, there can be misuse of the sprint burndown. Following are some common problems organizations experience when understanding and acting upon the information in sprint burndowns.

The Microscope

The Problem

Early Scrum literature emphasized the sprint burndown as the main tool for establishing project health. At that time, it was encouraged to share the sprint burndown freely throughout the organization as a way to promote project transparency. But when teams did this, they found themselves on the receiving end of a lot of questions. Often managers and other stakeholders, particularly those who had not yet embraced agile thinking, overanalyzed these charts. Every anomaly was subject to review, and teams found themselves having to explain, for example, why the burndown appeared not to move for a day or two. Not surprisingly, in these organizations, sharing the sprint burndown seemed to create more problems than it solved. Teams felt as though they were under a microscope with their every movement needing to be explained.

Why This Happens

Stakeholders misinterpret the sprint burndown for usually a couple of reasons. First, they are often making assumptions about what patterns within the graph mean when those assumptions may not be true at all. For example, it is not unusual for a sprint burndown to "flatline" for short periods, meaning go completely horizontal. Stakeholders may misinterpret this to mean that no work is getting done. But that isn't necessarily true. It may simply mean the team is working through a particularly tough bit of the user story. If they are still defining the problem or exploring possible solutions to a given technical issue, it is not at all unusual that the burndown flatlines for a time. Stakeholders who don't understand this may want to step in and take action when, in reality, this may be completely unnecessary.

The amount of work remaining in a sprint burndown chart can be tracked in a number of different units, depending on what would be most useful for the team to see. Hours of work remaining, number of tasks, and even story points remaining are all common units of measurement on the Y-axis of a sprint burndown chart. When teams track hours of work remaining or number of tasks, it is not unusual to see that number go up before it goes down. Again, this reflects the exploratory nature of the first few days of the sprint. Team members learn as much as they can about the work involved before they start a sprint. But it is natural that, once they actually start creating the product, more information will be revealed. Often this new information is represented with additional time or additional tasks. An experienced team knows this can and probably will happen and will have taken it into consideration when making the sprint commitment. It is rarely a cause for worry.

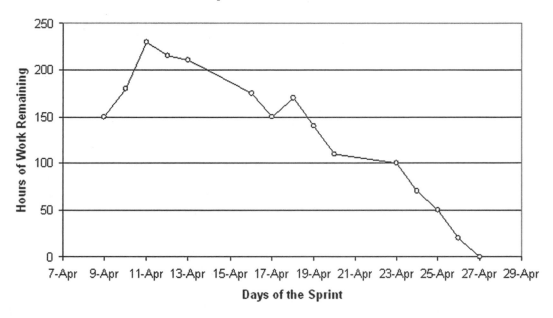

Sprint Burndown

But stakeholders who do not understand this become very nervous when they see a burndown chart go up. In their minds, this represents a problem. The team missed something in their initial estimates. Again, we have the case of the wrong thing being emphasized. Stakeholders may fret over the burndown going briefly upward when this trend may be no threat whatsoever to the sprint commitment. This reaction reveals that they are still in "monitoring mode" and do not yet trust the team to take responsibility for delivering as promised.

The Fix

More recent Scrum literature emphasizes the fact the sprint burndown is primarily a tool for the Scrum inner circle. Stakeholders may believe a sprint burndown chart indicates dire problems when so often this simply is not true. The irony is the time the team will spend answering questions and defending themselves against overanxious stakeholders concerns can be a huge time-sink and one that legitimately does endanger the sprint.

WEEK 4

Even when the burndown reflects a true problem, stakeholders (and particularly managers) need to remember that this is the team's problem to fix, not theirs. Teams will not take ownership of their sprint commitment if someone is constantly jumping in to manipulate it. Missing sprint commitments will create the need for some serious, sometimes uncomfortable, discussions between the team, Product Owner, and ScrumMaster. This communication is rarely improved by the inclusion of outsiders. It is ultimately up to the Scrum inner circle to decide what information the sprint burndown yields and what to do about it.

The Quota Fillers

The Problem

Sprint burndowns give an at-a-glance look into how much work a team has left to deliver in their sprint commitment. As we've said before, commitments are at a team level. Even when the work divides out such that an individual on the team does most or all of the work for a given story, the commitment to deliver that story is borne by the whole team.

This "all for one, one for all" ethos sometimes does not sit well with non-Scrum managers. Used to monitoring individuals' performance, these managers can feel at a loss when it comes to determining how to judge the performance of a Scrum team member. So they come up with a suggestion to remedy this problem. Instead of, or in addition to, doing a team burndown, they want to do individual burndowns that show the amount of work remaining for each person on the team. Non-Scrum managers may have a quota of work they expect each person on the Scrum team to fill, often mapping in some fashion to the hours of time they have available. In the minds of these managers, doing individual burndowns is a solution to understanding each person's performance and value within the group.

Why This Happens

By now, we should recognize behavior patterns like this as typical of people who have not yet fully embraced agile values. To be fair, stakeholders, like managers, are often not as far along the agile learning curve as the Scrum inner circle. All they know are the tools and techniques they have used in the past. And they may not realize the damage they can cause in a fledgling Scrum team by continuing these practices.

But, needless to say, this type of oppressive monitoring clashes violently with Scrum and agile principles. It emphasizes the individual over the team and inhibits the shared commitment of Scrum. It will also make the team feel micromanaged as they are, once again, forced to account for every hour spent. One of the things team members say they like best about Scrum is that, once they make their sprint commitment, they are left alone to work in peace and decide together how best to meet that commitment. This level of trust makes them feel both valued and trusted. Individual burndowns have just the opposite effect. Team members may resort to filling their time with busy work to show managers they are adding value to the sprint. Teams subjected to individual burndowns quickly grow to hate Scrum as they see it as "just another way to micromanage us."

The Fix

Organizations should never do individual burndowns—period. When they do so, they are misusing the tool and setting their entire agile transformation up for failure. But managers in an organization moving to Scrum do have a dilemma. If they cannot track individual performance the way they used to, how do they track it? Scrum team members, like all teams, occasionally have performance problems. How can managers learn about and address these problems in a culture that emphasizes the team?

The answer is to turn to the team itself. No one knows the true value a Scrum team member provides better than his teammates. Peer reviews are an excellent way for managers to incorporate feedback from Scrum team members into the review process. Scrum teams are under intense pressure to deliver on commitments, so carrying someone on the team who does not pull his or her weight is not usually something they tolerate. That being said, the value individual team members bring to the group is not something that can always be measured in the lines of code they generate. Attitude, decision-making style, and temperament all contribute to a Scrum team member's value. Giving the team a forum (through peer reviews) to share this information gives a manager far more insight into an individual team member's contribution than a micromanaged burndown ever can.

WEEK 4

Likewise, when serious performance problems do occur, managers should expect to hear about them from the Scrum team itself, either through individual members or through the ScrumMaster in the form of raising an impediment. A Scrum team is a fairly autonomous, self-governing group. When they make a good-faith effort to work with a team member, and for whatever reason, that person is just not working out, they should have the ability to request that person be removed from the team. Ignoring such requests or responding to them with more individual monitoring only inhibits the team's ability to self-manage and makes them feel they do not have the support of the organization in doing Scrum.

The Air-brushed Beauty

The Problem

As we've seen, an important factor in understanding sprint burndown charts is to not overanalyze minor ups and downs in the curve. These graphs may flatline or even go up occasionally. Such minor anomalies do not necessarily mean the sprint is in danger.

But sometimes a team's burndown will reflect exactly the opposite. As they report the work completed each day of the sprint, miraculously they produce a burndown that drops at a perfectly even slope. If there are ten days in the sprint and two hundred hours of work to be done, exactly twenty hours of work gets reported as done each day. This is wonderful, right? Surely it must mean we have a team that has done perfect estimates and then is delivering flawlessly on those estimates.

Unfortunately, the answer is usually no. Teams that have perfect burndowns every sprint are often not reporting what they are really doing each day of the sprint but what they think the ScrumMaster and Product Owner want to hear. Like a photo spread in a magazine, they touch up their reports in the daily Scrum to make them look better. This deception can go unnoticed by the ScrumMaster and Product Owner—until a sprint where things go seriously wrong. When that happens, they are in for a rude surprise. Their perfect burndown looks great—right up until the day the whole sprint falls apart and the team is unable to deliver on their commitments.

Why This Happens

Teams that "airbrush" their sprint burndowns are often not being allowed to truly self-manage. They may be getting pressure to show how efficiently they are using the hours available. They may also be pushed to "estimate accurately." Their success may be measured not in whether they met their sprint commitment but if given user stories and tasks took exactly as long as they said they would. It is damaging enough when this pressure comes from managers and other stakeholders. But sometimes this message comes from a misguided ScrumMaster or Product Owner. When the team lacks support of those inside the Scrum inner circle, it is not surprising they resort to giving a glossed-over version of what is really going on in the sprint. Their attitude is, "We're going to tell you want you want to hear so you will leave us alone and let us get our work done."

The Fix

If a ScrumMaster suspects a team is glossing over the data in their sprint burndown, the first thing she should do is make certain neither she nor the Product Owner is inadvertently causing this behavior. There are two keys ways to do this. First, she can emphasize that meeting the sprint commitment is what really matters. Once a team makes a commitment, the ScrumMaster and Product Owner should make it clear they trust the team to decide how best to approach delivering on that commitment. They are there to help by removing impediments and clarifying requirements, not to micromanage the team's work. The Product Owner, in particular, should emphasize to the team the value he places on knowing sooner, rather than later, when problems come up in a sprint. One way to get early visibility into such issues is through having a sprint burndown that accurately reflects the current state of the sprint.

A second way to support the team's right to self-manage is simply to stop estimating tasks in hours at all. Many teams take to relative estimation very quickly and will rapidly move to estimating their user stories with a T-shirt-size scale or something similar. But these same teams are often pressured to keep estimating the tasks themselves in hours. Teams quickly find these two estimating efforts redundant and rightly so. If they know enough about the size of a user story to accept it into a sprint, taking the time to

WEEK 4

estimate individual tasks often yields little or no extra value. Indeed, the only people who seem to make use of these estimates of hours are managers and other parties who continue to micromanage a team. Eliminating completely estimates in hours and reporting a sprint burndown only in number of tasks remaining or story points remaining is a tangible step in making a team feel safe enough to give honest feedback about sprint progress.

Managing the Release

As we've seen, sprint burndown charts give useful clues as to the health of a given sprint. But Product Owners often want and need to do longer-range planning. They need to know not just how the current sprint is going but also the progress of the overall project. They need to be able to answer to management such questions as:

- When is the current release going to be ready for delivery?
- What features will be in the release?
- How are additions and changes to scope affecting the delivery date?

To provide answers, the Product Owner must look beyond the results of a single sprint. He must develop a new way of monitoring and managing projects that takes into account the fact that requirements will emerge along the way. Most Product Owners discover that, when they begin managing their projects in an agile way, their processes for initiating and monitoring projects must also change.

One tool that Product Owners and organizations can use to understand the health of an entire release is a release burndown chart. Similar to the sprint burndown, this tool can help indicate the progress of an entire release, which may include several sprints. As we see below, the format is much the same as a sprint burndown. The Y-axis illustrates the amount of work remaining. But this now represents the amount of work remaining in the entire release. The X-axis represents the sprints themselves.

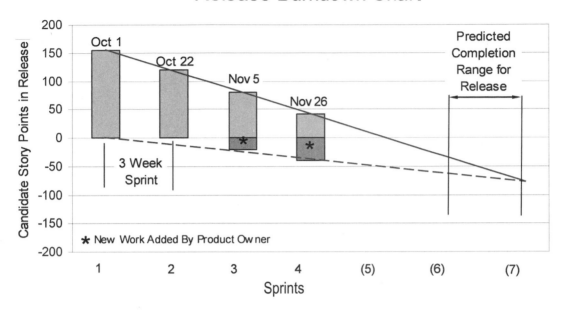

As you can see, it is possible to indicate with a trend line the average rate at which the graph is dropping. This represents the average rate at which the team is delivering work. But what happens when the Product Owner adds new work? That is presented by adding to the graph below the X-axis, as has occurred in Sprint 3, above. These additions can be tracked cumulatively from sprint to sprint. In doing so, this artifact now conveys two important pieces of information about this release: the average rate at which the team is delivering work and the average rate at which the Product Owner is adding new work. By extrapolating trend lines for both, it is possible to use this information to predict when the project will be done.

The information gained from a release burndown can be very illuminating. Some projects, if they were graphed on this chart, would show that their two trend lines would never meet! In such cases, based on the rate the team completes work and the rate the Product Owner adds new work, the project would never be done. Seeing this information in graphical form can be a wake-up call for a Product Owner who constantly heaps on new work, still hoping magically to meet a fixed date.

WEEK 4

The release burndown is a very useful tool for agile project management. But, beyond the use of any specific tool, managing agile projects often requires a change of mindset. Managing an agile project is an exercise in making tradeoffs and staying in "reality land." In other words, instead of threatening or cajoling a team to somehow make the impossible happen, a good Product Owner knows that any project is a series of tradeoffs. By knowing what is really most important to the organization's goals, he can use these tradeoffs to deliver as much value as possible with the time and money available.

If an organization has a history of poor project management, this may not instantly go away once an agile approach is used. Indeed, Scrum is particularly adept at exposing how ineffective these approaches really are. Below are some of the common problems organizations may have with agile project management and release planning.

The Alternate Universe

The Problem

Product Owners and other leaders in the enterprise often find themselves under extreme pressure to make up-front promises about when projects will be done. Particularly in organizations that serve outside clients, contracts may be written and dates and sets of features agreed to before anyone on the project team has had time to develop a sense of what is truly being asked for. To compound this problem, new requirements almost always emerge along the way, making the original estimates obsolete. Understanding what is truly fixed in a project—for example, a project that is date-driven—is crucial in helping a Product Owner work with clients to make intelligent tradeoffs in project deliverables.

Unfortunately, some organizations have a history of making promises to clients and then leaving it to the team to figure out how to deliver on them. Often, when such organizations move to an agile approach, they do not stop this behavior. They support the team's right to self-manage—so long as that self-management delivers exactly the amount of work they promised the clients and exactly on the date they promised it. Their attitude is, "I told the client we would deliver this in four months. You can commit to however much work you want in each sprint … as long as everything is done in four months." Such directives may come from the Product Owner or from an outside entity, such as a manager. But in either case, the problem is that the amount of work requested may have no relation to what can actually be accomplished in the given time period. Rather than working with the team to understand what is really possible, leaders who give such directives are attempting to change the laws of physics. They live in a mental alternative universe where they can wish a twelve-month project into a four-month timeslot simply because that is what they desire. Such projects often fail spectacularly, and when they do, the team is left to explain why they, once again, let the organization down.

Why This Happens

Product Owners and other leaders who make no effort to link their customer promises to what is actually within the realm of the possible are not yet thinking in an agile way. They may attempt to get the team to commit to delivering everything the customer wants by a given date. But they forget this is not the responsibility of the team in an agile approach like Scrum. The team makes commitments on a sprint-by-sprint basis only. Of course, a good Product Owner will certainly consult the team to get their opinion as to whether, for example, delivering a given set of features by a particular date is even reasonable. But when the answer to that question is no, it falls not to the team but to the Product Owner to decide next steps. Often this means hard discussions with stakeholders in an effort to either adjust schedule or reduce scope. These difficult conversations are part of the Product Owner's job. It is his responsibility to work with stakeholders to help them understand what is possible. Simply making promises up front and then leaving it to the team to figure out how to do the impossible means the Product Owner is not fulfilling his part of the bargain.

The Fix

When a Product Owner lays out a set of features for a release, he should realize those user stories represent a wish list. Until he consults with the team, he has no way of knowing if the amount of work involved in delivering those features is remotely reasonable within the time constraints of the schedule. Even after work on the release begins, a good Product Owner is always prepared for things to go wrong. When that happens, he knows he must be

WEEK 4

ready to make tradeoffs. This is one reason why the product backlog must always be in priority order. That way, if time runs short and not all desired features can be included in the release, the Product Owner can look to the last few user stories as items that could potentially be moved to another release.

Product Owners can help other leaders in the organization develop this tradeoff mindset. One way to do this is through project reporting. If a team has estimated all the PBIs in a given release, the Product Owner can refer to that metric as the "candidate story-point total." By doing so, he says, in effect, "This story-point total represents all the PBIs I hope to get in this release. The actual number may differ, depending on the results of each sprint." Then, each sprint, he can report on progress. For example, below is a typical management status report for a Scrum project:

Release 5 Status Report as of June 11	
Start Date:	May 1
End Date:	June 23
Total Release Candidate Story Points:	180
Story Points Completed:	78
Team's Average Velocity:	26
Average New Story Points Added per Sprint:	6

Agile Tip

Release burndowns are much more useful to stakeholders, like management, than sprint burndowns are. They give valuable information about the health of the project.

As you can see, many of these metrics are those that go into creating the release burndown. It can be useful to create status reports or even an executive dashboard that has both the release burndown and the data that goes into it. Having this information available during status meetings with management gives the Product Owner ammunition for arguing against unrealistic expectations. For example, using these metrics, he can show that the team has produced a regular velocity of twenty-six story points a sprint for multiple sprints. If the promises made to customers require a velocity of fifty-five story points per sprint, having this data at hand can help show that there is no evidence this is possible. Then the Product Owner can work with management to make intelligent tradeoffs that yield the most value possible.

Product Owners who work with external clients may have some educating to do. Of course, if a client is absolutely not interested in working in an agile way, it may be hard to convince him to partake in these tradeoff discussions. But the agile methods are gaining popularity in all sectors of business. Many requests for proposals state that respondents must to able to perform work using agile methods like Scrum. Product Owners with external clients will find more of them than ever open to create contracts that support working in an agile way.

When working with external clients, the key is to remember and emphasize the benefits agile brings to them. In traditional project management, when clients and outside partners, such as consulting agencies, engage in work, a requirements document is created and signed up front, before any development work is done. After that, any changes to the list of requirements requires a signed client-change-request, or CCR, and additional cost. But with Scrum, clients can make tradeoffs. They can substitute backlog items of similar size for one another with no cost penalty. This can be a very appealing benefit to clients who have gotten stuck in the past, paying for features that, in the end, they didn't need. And if money unexpectedly runs out near the end of the project, they can simply leave off features at the bottom of the product backlog. They are not stuck paying simply because they signed a contract months earlier.

Product Owners must always remember their job is about weighing costs and benefits and making tradeoffs. In organizations, as in life in general, people tend to have more wants and needs than they have time or money. So making the best use of all resources available should be the goal. Rather than making empty promises and then leaving it up to the team to figure out how to deliver, Product Owners and other leaders should work to understand what is possible. Doing so provides the best chance of delivering what has been promised in the time available.

WEEK 4

The Big Bang

The Problem

Deciding the candidate user stories to include in a release is often a multi-step process. First the Product Owner will work with stakeholders to prioritize the items for the product backlog. Then, he will often ask the team to provide high-level estimates for all user stories he is considering for the release. After estimation, he may shuffle the list yet again, often moving items up or down, based on the effort they will require to complete. And even after work begins, in each sprint, he has the opportunity to make refinements, adding, subtracting, or moving backlog items.

Using relative estimation, a team can work with the Product Owner in one or more Story-Time sessions to estimate all the PBIs in a given release. But doing so will sometimes require that organizations redefine what constitutes a release. For many enterprises, this term already has a meaning. It is often associated with the end of the project and may constitute many months of work. While Scrum teams can use techniques, like T-shirt sizing to quickly estimate a few dozen items, when the list grows to a few hundred items, this grows impractical. When Product Owners create releases that are too long—for example, twelve months—they inhibit the team's ability to estimate the whole release. They also lose one of the best advantages of Scrum: frequent releases to the customer.

Why This Happens

This "big bang" approach is almost always a leftover from waterfall thinking. Product Owners may equate a release with the end of the project. They may still have the attitude that "until I have everything I want, the entire system is useless." But, of course, this is not true. Even after sprints when no release is planned, giving the stakeholders an opportunity to see and comment on the product can yield important feedback. And it is better still when they can actually begin using it. A useful increment of working product is what constitutes a release in Scrum, and it is an important inspect-and-adapt point in the project.

The Fix

As we've said before, there are many words in Scrum that have special meanings beyond their common usage. "Release" is one of those words. Product Owners must work with the team and stakeholders to determine what would constitute a meaningful body of work to include in a release. They must also define what it means to "release" something. This definition may vary from project to project.

For example, suppose a Scrum team is building a new customer-information system to replace an aging one. The organization may decide it is best to switch, or cut over, to the new system in production all at once. That doesn't mean, however, that incremental releases cannot be done. The organization may establish a second environment outside of production in which they can provide regular releases of the new system. Doing so provides many advantages. It allows the team and Product Owner to gather feedback from stakeholders, helps management understand project progress, and provides a place for users to gain familiarity with the new system.

As Product Owners become more experienced, they learn that frequency of inspect-and-adapt points is one of the key ways to manage risk in a Scrum project. Shorter sprints offer more frequent chances to readjust course. And so do shorter releases. Keeping releases to a moderate length will provide the Product Owner flexibility and help improve the overall predictability of the project. What constitutes "moderate length"? This will vary, depending upon the type of projects and products. But a good rule of thumb is if your release is more than three to four months long or more than seven to eight sprints, take a closer look to see if a shorter release schedule might be beneficial.

The Fire Hose

The Problem

Some teams take the opposite approach to big-bang releases. Knowing they can produce real, working product every sprint, they assume it would be ideal to also release every sprint. "Why wait?" they ask. "Our customers want this stuff, and they can use it, so why not release to them every sprint?" Of course, some organizations do release every sprint. This approach can work just fine if the whole enterprise can support it. But the team, ScrumMaster, and Product Owner must remember they are not the only ones with work to do in a release. The end users are ultimately the most affected by a release. They are the ones who have to learn how the new functionality works and use it day-to-day to do their jobs. Having new functionality to learn and adapt to every two weeks can be daunting for end users. Whereas, before Scrum, new features may have trickled slowly out to them with weeks of lead time, that flow of new features may now feel like a fire hose. If they are unable to keep up, they may turn against Scrum simply in an effort slow changes and allow them time to still get their work done.

Why This Happens

This is an interesting but common side-effect of working in an iterative fashion. Good Scrum teams can produce an astonishing amount of work. And while every organization wants productive teams, keeping up with the output of these super-workers can be daunting. It is a good problem to have—hyper-productive teams—but it is a problem nonetheless.

Sometimes these issues are caused by a simple lack of sensitivity to end users' schedules. For example, many departments in a typical organization have particular times of the year when they are extremely busy. For a finance department, that may be when they are doing year-end processes. For a human resources group, it might be during open enrollment, when employees make choices about benefits. And managers are almost always very busy during the time of the year when the annual review process takes place. Scrum teams should realize that frequent releases during these stressful periods may not be welcomed.

But if the organization protests frequent releases in general, what the Scrum team may be experiencing is the effect of being mid-process in a culture change. Often Scrum teams, along with the Product Owner and ScrumMaster, come to fully embrace an empirical approach to work. They consistently eliminate inefficient processes, improve transparency, and learn to work effectively as a unit. Unfortunately, they may find the rest of the organization is still doing work the way they always have. If long cycles and slow change was the norm before Scrum, it will take some time and effort to change those beliefs. Until others in the organization see value in making small, incremental changes, they may not be able to absorb releases as fast as the Scrum team can produce them.

The Fix

Product Owners should make an effort to work with their stakeholders to establish a release schedule that end users can handle. Any times of the year when releases should be minimized or avoided are best discovered up front, before they happen. But beyond this, the entire Scrum inner circle should realize that the best way to bring the benefits of agile to the organization is to get everyone working in that fashion. Scrum happened to be developed as a way to build software. But the principles on which it is based have far wider application. Until this way of thinking is spread throughout an organization, Scrum will remain something "the tech guys do." But when each person in the enterprise thinks in an empirical way—making small, incremental changes, weighing costs and benefits, prioritizing—an organization can truly begin to transform. Smaller, more frequent releases can become the norm. But until this shift in thinking takes place, Scrum teams must be patient. They were once Scrum novices too. They should remember this and not overwhelm their end-users with releases they cannot handle and do not want. Through education and results, they can often slowly bring the entire organization around to this new way of thinking and help the enterprise become truly agile.

> **Agile Tip**
>
> Be aware that frequent releases will be an adjustment for the user community. Be sensitive to the fact that they need some time to adjust to this new incremental way of working.

As we've seen, moving to an agile way of thinking requires more than simply behavior changes. It requires a fundamental mindset shift. Old ways of doing activities like estimating, monitoring performance, and measuring project health must often be revised. Doing so requires understanding *why* these approaches no longer suit the organization's needs. The Scrum team, ScrumMaster, and Product Owner should understand that these changes may take time. It is said that change happens one person at a time. And different people have different capacities for change. The best thing a Scrum inner circle can do is demonstrate on a daily basis the benefits of working in an agile way. Working at a sustainable pace, producing consistent results, making intelligent tradeoffs—these are all behaviors the rest of the organization

WEEK 4

can learn from and begin to model. When that happens, an organization is well on its way to agile transformation.

Week 5 – Creating an Action Plan

In Week 5 we'll create an action plan for moving forward. We'll assess where your organization is on the Agile Transformation scale and how they can move to the next level with your help.

If you've kept to the schedule laid out in this book, you've spent the last four weeks looking at some of the most common problems organizations experience when they try to adopt an agile method like Scrum. In reading about these issues, you may have discovered your agile transformation is going better than you thought. Maybe some of the problems others struggle with are issues you have already worked out. Or maybe you discovered (as you may have suspected) that you still have a long way to go before you can truly call your enterprise "agile." So now what? Where do you go from here, and how can you take what you've learned over the preceding pages and create an actionable plan?

In addition to understanding common pitfalls and problems with an implementation of agile practices, it can also be helpful to understand what agile transformation looks like. Agile transformations follow a "loosely predictable" path. This means that, while no transformation is identical to another, there are common patterns. A typical organization goes through the following phases as it steadily builds agility:

Non-agile Enterprise	Exploration	Coordination	Process Definition	Strategic Alignment	Transformation	Agile Enterprise

Let's take a moment to understand these phases better.

Exploration

The exploration phase of an agile implementation is marked by interest and the pursuit of knowledge. This is when one or more teams start to do some tentative exploration with agile concepts. They may read books and articles about agile. They learn about the popular agile frameworks, like Scrum and eXtreme Programming. They also usually send a few people to training to formalize their knowledge. People who attend my certified Scrum courses from organizations at this level of adoption often ask many hypothetical questions: "If this happened, what would be the right thing to do?" Their questions are hypothetical because they have not yet had the experience to expose a lot of impediments.

Two key factors for success in the exploration stage of an agile transformation are getting that experience and laying the groundwork for expansion.

They are related activities but not identical. If an organization chooses Scrum as their agile project-management framework, then getting experience means sending people to training and actually doing a few Scrum projects. Until the enterprise takes this step, all the problems they may experience exist only in their minds. And hypothetical problems are the hardest to solve because they exist only in the realm of theory. So a key factor, once an interest in agile and Scrum has been established, is to get some experience via pilot projects.

Laying the groundwork for expanding an agile transformation is more an exercise in salesmanship and politics. Even if they don't much like the status quo, many people view change with suspicion. The early Scrum pioneers in an organization should work to build support for agile practices. Start with easy wins. Look for people who are open to agile concepts. You may have some natural innovators in your enterprise—those people always interested in learning about the latest and greatest. These early adopters are natural allies in your quest to become agile. Together, you can build momentum. And look for those most unhappy with the current practices. These are people who are motivated to look for a better way.

Ideally, it is best to spread agile concepts through a "pull" rather than "push" approach. If people can volunteer to use Scrum rather than be forced to do so, they generally approach the process in a more open-minded state. Get a couple of teams doing Scrum. Use physical taskboards, if possible, to track sprint progress. Nothing sparks curiosity in a typical beige office environment like a wall covered with colorful Post-its. Interested individuals will be drawn to ask questions. And that initial interest can be the first step in *recruiting* others to the agile cause.

Coordination

By the time organizations have moved to the coordination phase of their agile adoption, they have done enough projects to have generated lots of impediments. Believe it or not, this is good thing. Until problems are identified, they cannot be removed. People who attend Scrum courses whose organizations are in this phase want to talk about real-world problems, not hypothetical ones. Unfortunately, this advanced-beginner stage is one where many organizations get stuck, not making appreciable improvements past this point. There is an "ah-ha" moment during the coordination phase when organizations realize, "Ugh—this agile stuff is hard!" And, like a fledgling exerciser after that first tough workout, their instinct can be to give up.

Two things can help greatly with this. First, the organization can start to build internal agile advocates. These are agile coaches within the organization whose job it is to teach, model, and spread agile values. They evangelize agile principles throughout the organization. It is these individuals that new teams will contact to learn how to get started with agile and where to go for training. And where do these agile advocates get their knowledge? From a professional agile coach. Especially in the case of large enterprises, this is the stage of agile adoption when onsite training and coaching is extremely valuable. An organization intent on a true transformation to agile should use this time to build a long-term relationship with an agile coach. The combination of experience and emotional distance these coaches provide can help organizations avoid needlessly making every beginner's mistake. Between using a professional coach and internal agile champions, an organization is well on their way to building a foundation for agile success.

But, just as important, there is a mindset shift that must start to take place in organizations moving to agile. They must realize that the object is not to fit agile into their existing practices but, rather, to design practices where using agile methods works naturally and easily. So often people will come to a Scrum training and ask something like: "How do I make Scrum fit into my current project-approval process?" The short answer I give is, "Ask a better quality question." What I mean by that is, rather than trying to fit Scrum into a process which may not even be serving the organization's needs, they should put some effort into thinking about what an effective process might look like. So a better version of the question above might be, "If our project-approval process worked perfectly with Scrum, what would it look like?" Granted, those changes might not happen overnight. But at least the end state they are trying to describe is not flawed from the beginning. Processes have a lifecycle. They are useful for a time, and then, as the business moves on, processes

> **Agile Tip**
>
> Pilot projects tend to be more successful when employees have been trained in Scrum. Organizations that make the effort to send representatives from each of the Scrum roles to training tend to move more quickly towards agile transformation.

too must change. As organizations move through the coordination phase of agile adoption, they may find themselves questioning nearly every process they have! Rigid organizational boundaries may be challenged as well. This effort can be painful, but it is necessary. Having these conversations is a big step towards creating transparency in the organization.

Process Definition

By the time an organization has moved to the process-definition stage of transformation, they, in large part, understand what being agile is about. This isn't some fad they are trying because the CEO read about it in a magazine article. This is simply the way they get work done. Agile project management methods like Scrum move from being the exception to being the rule. And this new norm requires new processes and tools to support it. Organizations in this stage begin to do things like rewrite job descriptions to reflect Scrum roles. They work with the project-management office to change the way projects are approved and initiated. And they buy tools that let them manage projects in an agile way, rather than try to push agile projects into tools meant for traditional project management.

Ironically, organizations in process definition are often extremely critical of themselves. When I come in to coach these groups, they say, "We still aren't very good at Scrum—we are doing so many things wrong!" Simply the fact that they see and acknowledge this tells me they are further along the agile evolution scale than the average company. A novice runner is thrilled he can simply finish a five-kilometer race. An experienced runner is disappointed at that same event if his time is ten seconds slower than expected. The difference in attitude of these individuals comes from knowing what is possible. Like the experienced runner, organizations in process definition see not only how far they have come but also how far they have yet to go. Their standards and expectations have been raised.

This awareness can cause discouragement. One way organizations can manage this transition and also spread learning about agile concepts is to tell their story. Enterprises that have made it this far in an agile implementation have already exceeded what the average company accomplishes when implementing agile. They have also, no doubt, gotten solid and measurable benefits from these practices. Case studies and conference presentations

WEEK 5

give them a chance to articulate those benefits. These opportunities to share accomplish two things. First, they help promote learning in the agile community. Often, just hearing that someone has done something before you makes you think you also can do it. But it will also give the presenting organization a new perspective. They will realize just how far they have come. I remember, early in my agile career, attending a Scrum event where the speaker kicked off the session with this statement: "I know no one is really doing Scrum yet, but does anyone have plans to start?" At the time, I had been doing Scrum for almost eight months in multiple projects. I had experience in both the Product Owner and ScrumMaster role. My immediate reaction was, "Wow—I probably know more about this stuff than anyone in this room." When organizations publish case studies and present at conferences, they get a different view into their knowledge level. Doing so can provide the impetus they need to continue to improve.

Strategic Alignment

Up to this point, planning in an organization is often managed with two distinct and completely separate efforts. One, tactical planning, such as determining the work in a daily Scrum or even monitoring a release comprised of several sprints, is something the Scrum inner circle likely manages very well. At any given time, any Scrum team member could tell you not only what he is working on in a given day but also how that work contributes to both the current sprint and the upcoming release.

But there is another planning effort that goes on, and it happens at a much higher, strategic level. This is where organizational leaders decide overall product and portfolio goals. They determine where, as an organization, they want to be in the marketplace. They may also set revenue goals. When an organization reaches the stage of strategic alignment, they realize these two planning efforts can no longer be done independently of one another. Strategic goals must feed into tactical goals, with the whole process being tightly coupled.

Being able to do this requires those who do the strategic planning, often high-level managers, to understand and adopt an agile mindset. They must understand what agile teams need from them. First, they need product and project goals. Teams need to understand what the target is at which they are aiming. Once they do, they can work with the Product Owner to determine how best to meet those goals. Agile managers must also understand their role is no longer to monitor and oversee but, instead, to remove impediments. They should expect and welcome hearing about impediments, knowing that every problem resolved moves the enterprise one step closer to working in a fluid, agile way.

Organizations in strategic alignment also begin to see marked interest in trying Scrum outside the realm of technology projects. At first the questions may be tentative: "I know this is kind of crazy, but do you think we could use Scrum to set up the new warehouse?" With encouragement and help from internal agile advocates, these fledgling groups can begin using Scrum and other agile methods to manage their own projects. This is yet another step on the path of internalizing agile values. Scrum and other agile methods become simply a way of thinking and a way of getting work done. When an enterprise has reached this point, they are well on their way to agile transformation.

> **Agile Tip**
>
> At some point, other groups in the organization may become interested in using Scrum for some of their projects. This is a good sign that the entire organization is starting to internalize agile values.

Transformation

A beautiful thing happens when organizations achieve agile transformation. Agile values become internalized, not just in the Scrum teams but also throughout the organization. Individuals and enterprises who reach this stage simply think differently. When I speak with team members who have fully internalized these values, they say, "I just couldn't go back to the old way of doing things now. I see why that approach didn't work and why an agile approach does. It is just how I do my work now."

When this happens, agile has become the new "normal." Agile behaviors and thought patterns become the rule rather than the exception. New hires are chosen because they already fit into an agile culture. Agile becomes the expectation. Like a process of evolution, these values become more ingrained in the corporate mindset.

Organizations at this stage of adoption are not free of problems. Particularly with large enterprises, they may have teams that are very agile and

WEEK 5

teams that struggle. But individuals in an agile organization see problems—and opportunities—much sooner, and more important, they see them for what they are. This vision allows an agile enterprise to respond to such situations both faster and more effectively. Individuals in an agile organization believe the right path always exists, so the question becomes not *if* something can be done but *how*. And that is a much more empowering approach to problem-solving.

Plotting a Course for Change

So, given the path to agile transformation and the problems we learned in the last section that block an organization's advancement along this path, what skills should we focus on at each level? Below is a graphic that shows when it would be most advantageous to master each skill set:

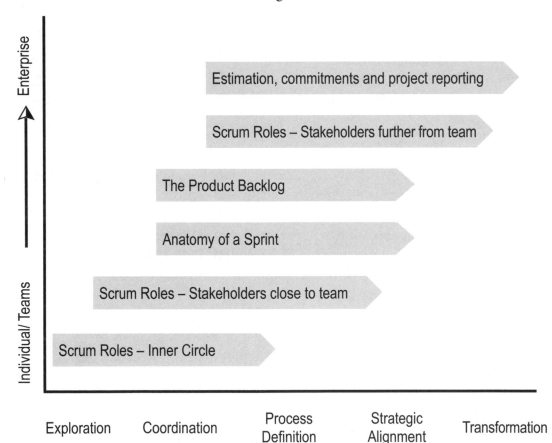

As you can see, everything starts with the Scrum inner circle understanding and performing their roles well. Until that happens, there is no point focusing on more advanced issues. Engaging key stakeholders should be the next goal—those closest to the Scrum inner circle or those with a great deal of influence—with a broader set of stakeholders coming on board later. Then the organization must get good at the mechanics of Scrum: holding effective planning meetings, building actionable product backlogs, doing regular backlog-grooming sessions. Practicing these activities often enough to be good at them is a bit like practicing scales when learning to play the piano: not all that fun but something that definitely pays dividends down the road.

Only when these fundamental skills are there should an organization worry about doing a lot of long-range planning, project monitoring, and scaling. Too often, I come into organizations that say, "Can you help us scale Scrum over twenty teams with members distributed across three continents?" Yet these same organizations cannot run a single sprint-planning meeting effectively. It is important to walk before you try to run. Taking the time to get good at the basics of Scrum will build a solid foundation for further advancements.

Go through the problems identified in the previous section and decide which ones affect your organization the most. Choose one or two of those problems to focus on improving. Start with problems that are in the lower left portion of the graph above. In other words, don't worry so much about getting stakeholders on board if your Scrum inner circle doesn't even know what is expected of them. First things first. Build a strong base, and the later stages of agile adoption will flow much more smoothly.

In Scrum projects, as in life, there are problems, and then there are "problems." So how do you know the difference? How do you know if a behavior is a simple learning-curve issue or the symptom of a deeper disconnect? Some challenges an organization will face while implementing Scrum are natural bumps in the road when learning a new way of working. For example, new Product Owners often write user stories that are too large or too vague. This is natural in the beginning when they are just learning to write requirements in a user-story format. Practice and help from the team and ScrumMaster will fix this over time. But a Product Owner who is absent and doesn't take the job seriously is a red flag. Until this individual gets more engaged, she can't even get on the learning curve, much less ascend it.

We've learned that success with an agile implementation centers around individuals and organizations developing a threefold approach to their agile practice: understanding what to do, how to do it well, and why to do it. Once the organization understands these factors, only the actual doing is left.

So how do you know if you have a serious flaw in your agile implementation? Below are a set of red flags, an Agile Dirty Dozen. Many of the problems we identified in this book are symptomatic expressions of these deeper problems. If you see these behaviors or trends in your organization, they indicate that the individuals involved not only don't know how to effectively be agile but also simply do not understand the underlying principles of agility. Fixing these issues will require not only changes in behavior but also in beliefs. If you hope to see agile practices grow and thrive in your organization, watch for these fundamental flaws.

The Agile Dirty Dozen
Roles

1. Teams that don't self-manage

The cornerstone of all agile product development is the self-managed team. The principle behind this is that the collective creativity and intelligence of a group will ultimately produce a better solution than the ideas of any one person, no matter how smart or well-informed that individual is. Teams must self-manage in order for an organization to reap the benefits of agile. As we've seen in this book, initiating this process can be a little more complicated than just telling a team, "OK, go forth and self-manage!" The team must feel it is safe to self-manage. Sometimes they must be reminded how to self-manage and work together as a unit. They must also see evidence their management will let them self-manage. Until this support structure is in place, the organization will not feel like a place where self-management is welcomed.

2. Product Owners who don't or can't fulfill their role

It is amazing to me how many product companies in the world have, effectively, no one taking responsibility for their product lines. The Scrum team's job is greatly simplified by a strong Product Owner. When I say "strong," I do not mean this person is authoritative and directive. A good Product Owner has a unique blend of personality characteristics that makes him ideally suited to the job. A good Product Owner can make decisions quickly but never makes them in a vacuum. He knows resources are limited so he harbors no illusions that tradeoffs will be unnecessary. He works closely with stakeholders and the Scrum team but knows ultimately that he is responsible for making certain the right product gets built. And he has the support of management to make these tough decisions. When the Product Owner doesn't have this level of investment in his product, his ability to do well in this role is severely impaired.

3.   ScrumMasters who act like managers (or overprotective parents)

Since the ScrumMaster role exists only in the Scrum framework, the person coming to this job has inevitably had other roles in the past. Some of the traits and characteristics from those other assignments will serve them well in the ScrumMaster role. And some will not. The key to this individual being successful in the role is to understand which traits are useful to the ScrumMaster role and which are not.

Perhaps one of the most difficult things for some ScrumMasters to learn is that it is not their job to make anyone do anything. ScrumMasters must have the courage to watch a failure in progress. This is particularly true within the Scrum inner circle. True, a ScrumMaster can make observations, ask questions, and offer suggestions. Perhaps a Scrum team has committed to fifty story points for two sprints in a row but only delivered thirty each time. Yet they insist "this time will be different." So be it. The ScrumMaster must be willing to stand back and watch the team attempt what is almost certainly an unrealistic sprint commitment yet again. And, just as important, she must not step up to explain away the failure to management, the Product Owner, or customers. Let the team do that. No doubt, this will be an uncomfortable experience for them. Negative reinforcement is a powerful teacher. Only by letting the team experience the consequences of their actions will they learn from the experience.

4. Stakeholders who don't play by the rules

There is a difference between wanting to start a fitness program and *wanting to want* to start a fitness program. The first produces results. The second may produce some half-hearted actions—signing up for a gym, buying running shoes—but little if anything comes of it. The difference is the level of commitment. When stakeholders—especially customers and managers—hear about Scrum, they are often all for it. Who doesn't want high-producing teams and Product Owners that take responsibility for the time and money they spend? But often stakeholders forget this universal truth: you don't get something for nothing. Yes, their Scrum teams can be highly productive, but not without their help and support. When stakeholders agree to take part in Scrum, their first question to the team should be, "How can we support this and help you succeed?" Stakeholders who think they will receive the benefits of Scrum without changing their own behavior to support Scrum principles are a little like those people who think they will start losing those extra pounds from having a gym membership without doing any workouts. Getting good at Scrum takes effort from everyone in the organization. Until stakeholders internalize this idea, they likely won't realize the extent to which their own behavior needs to change.

Mechanics

5. Organizations that do not understand or value commitments

Some recent Scrum literature has softened the idea of a commitment into a forecast. While I think I understand the motivation behind this change, nonetheless, it disappoints me. Having spent years as a Product Owner, one of the key benefits I saw from Scrum was the fact that the team made commitments to me. And I, in turn, could make commitments to management and customers. True, sometimes those commitments were not delivered. But most of the Scrum teams I worked with took the idea of commitment very seriously.

I also knew that, in extracting commitments from my team, I was making commitments to them as well. For example, I committed to not introducing new backlog items mid-sprint. I knew if I did that our original agreement would need to be renegotiated.

Organizations, and perhaps people in general, need to rediscover the value of commitment. Do you remember the time when a handshake was as good as a contract, when a person's word of honor was enough to seal a business deal? Some of those old-fashioned values work very nicely in the new world of agility as well. Organizations that do well with agile principles are filled with individuals that trust one another. They often have deep personal relationships. And because of this, they take commitments seriously. Scrum teams make commitments to Product Owners. Product Owners make commitments to stakeholders. And management makes commitments to help remove impediments. Until everyone in the organization understands that commitments are a two-way street, agile may be seen like another way to squeeze more work out of a team.

6. Organizations that cannot timebox

There is a myth that making good decisions always takes a long time. In fact, when evaluating a problem and developing potential solutions, there comes a point of diminishing returns. This is one of the fundamental principles behind the idea of time-boxing. Another principle behind time-boxing is that it is useful to be able to work within time constraints because often those constraints are outside your control. Think back to the last time you flew on a commercial aircraft. If your flight left at, for example, 11:05 a.m., you had the earlier part of your morning to timebox your travel preparations. But whether you are ready at that time or not, that flight is leaving on schedule at 11:05 a.m., with or without you.

Organizations new to agile may struggle with time-boxing. They may complain, "Everything would have been fine if we had just had more time." But this is rarely the case. Instead, they must learn to use well the time they have available. It is a different way of thinking but very powerful once it is internalized. In a highly competitive world, the ability to maximize the use of scarce resources is a talent worth having. And no resource is more scarce than time. Until enterprises see that they must treat time like the precious resource it is, it will be hard for them to reap the full benefits of agility.

WEEK 5

7. **Organizations that don't make full use of the inspect-and-adapt process**

Humans are adept problem-solvers. We are very good at working around obstacles. Unfortunately, we are also creatures of patterns and habits. Sometimes, we forget that obstacles don't always have to be worked around. Some simply need to be removed.

This is the kind of mindset we need when we approach the inspect-and-adapt process. If an organization has fallen into the habit of giving lip service to activities like continuous improvement, they need to remind themselves what that really means. The inspect-and-adapt process is the engine that makes agile work. The perfect way to do something today may not be the perfect way to do it tomorrow. A person who has internalized the idea of inspect-and-adapt is always looking for refinements in the process, large or small, that bring better results. The agile mindset says, "Let's try it and see what happens."

Some ideas are successful—some aren't. Agile organizations feel differently about failure than those which are non-agile. "Failure" is simply an action that yielded information, which can be used to plan more actions. For a model of this kind of thought, we need look no further than Thomas Edison who said this about failure: "I am not discouraged because every wrong attempt discarded is another step forward."

8. **Organizations that neglect to give everyone the agile toolkit**

When an enterprise is just getting started with agile, it is not unusual that they have only a few people who truly understand how it works and what agile aspires to achieve. But if wide-scale organizational benefits from agile are to be achieved, that must change. Everyone must get the "agile toolkit"—both the training to know how to use the agile frameworks and the chance to get experience.

Who is often neglected in an organization's quest to move to agile transformation? The Product Owners, geographically distributed teams, and outside entities, like partners, customers, and contractors. Too often, these individuals and groups are given a hasty explanation of what's expected from them in the agile processes. They are often told what to do but not why to do it. Because of this oversight, they won't understand whether they are getting good results or not. Every major player in an agile project must have a strong understanding of what the process is trying to produce and what the tools are that help create those results. Organizations that don't make an effort to do this run the risk of alienating people to the agile methods because they have too many negative experiences.

Culture and Belief Systems

9. Thinking of agile as "something the technology people do"

Scrum was originally created to help software development teams. And it is possible to get incremental improvements by simply using the framework to do technology projects. But Scrum and the other agile methods were built on principles like trust and collaboration. If the entire organization does not hold these values as important, and if these values are not reflected in their behaviors, conflict is certain to arise.

When organizations think of agile as "something the technology people do," they often underestimate the amount of change that must occur. Scrum and the other agile methods are not quick fixes. Doing daily meetings and working in sprints will not make your problems magically go away. Until an enterprise realizes that a move to agile will affect every part of the business, they will be agile in name only.

10. Understanding what behavior you are reinforcing

Every interaction between two or more people is a learning experience. Each person is storing away valuable information about the other for future use. Indeed, good ScrumMasters, in particular, learn a great deal about their teams simply from watching them work together.

However, this constant learning can cause problems when people don't realize what behaviors they are reinforcing. This can happen when a person says one thing but his actions convey something different. A Product Owner may encourage a team to let him know early when problems occur in the sprint. But if, when they do this, he attacks them verbally or otherwise makes them feel threatened, all he has accomplished is to teach them to keep bad news from him until the last possible moment.

When a ScrumMaster extends a sprint planning meeting because the team could not arrive at a sprint commitment, she has not helped them learn how to use time well but instead taught them to ask for extensions. When management extols the virtues of agile and self-managed teams but continues to micromanage each employee's work, team members know they are not really in control of their own commitments and, in response, do not self-manage.

The biggest danger here is that this disconnection between behavior and action can create a delusion throughout the organization about using agile. Such enterprises grow frustrated with their lack of success with it: "We're doing everything right. Why aren't we getting results?" they ask. What they have forgotten is the old adage, "Actions speak louder than words." People believe what you do, not what you say you do. Until the key players in the organization have good alignment with agile values in their actions as well as in their words, they will continue to generate behaviors in their agile teams that do not generate the desired agile results.

11. Understanding the art of the tradeoff

Forrest Gump's mother might think life is a box of chocolates, but good Product Owners know differently. For them, life is a series of costs and benefits. They are always evaluating: "How much will this cost me? What will I get for it? Is the cost commensurate with the benefit?" Not all costs—nor benefits, for that matter—can be measured in dollars. When you think about people you enjoy working with and those you don't, one important cost may be "headache factor." Some people, no matter how professionally brilliant, are just a pain to work with.

Organizations almost always have more wants than they do money or time to fulfill those wants, so tradeoffs must be made. In Scrum, the role of the Product Owner was developed to have a single point, that single "wringable neck," to make these tradeoff decisions. But the Product Owner can do this job only when he has the support of the organization.

When moving to agile, the entire organization must think, to a certain extent, a bit like a Product Owner. This is an especially important concept for managers to internalize. Because resources are limited but desires are not, good agile organizations master the art of the tradeoff. They have honest conversations about what are must-haves versus what can wait. And they don't delude themselves into believing something is possible simply because they want it to be so.

In non-agile organizations, teams are often told, "I know your regular velocity is thirty story points a sprint, but I promised the customer we'd deliver in May, so you'll need to find a way to bump it up to sixty." Leaders who do this can threaten and cajole the team all they want. What they cannot do is change the laws of physics. The only way a team can meet the new, higher target is through compromises in quality. They will pay back the time they borrowed from the original schedule (often several times over) in increased maintenance and clean-up efforts.

Good agile organizations stay in "reality land." Leaders is such organizations know intelligent tradeoffs will need to be made on almost every project. Product Owners understand the balance between schedule, features, and budget. They actively make choices about optimizing or controlling two of these features. But they know trying to control all three is folly. If budget and features are fixed and unchanging, then schedule must flex. If a project is date-driven (i.e., the schedule is fixed) and it has a limited budget, then the features that can be included are what must flex. To believe otherwise is to engage in self-delusion. Product Owners in agile organizations make proactive choices about these tradeoffs rather than pretending they don't need to happen.

12. Redefine success and celebrate it

Many software professionals have tales of projects where eighty-hour weeks and pulling all-nighters were the norm. In some ways (often in the glow of hindsight), the intensity of these projects can produce a kind of camaraderie among team members, not unlike soldiers on a battlefield. But the adrenaline rush of such frantic projects can be dangerously addictive. A whole organization can fall into a belief pattern that says, "If I don't see people rushing around madly and staying late to finish projects, they aren't working hard enough."

By contrast, an experienced agile team is a low-drama organization. Because teams and Product Owners work together closely to make realistic commitments and meet them, much of the behavior that was once rewarded in an organization—for example, pulling all-nighters to reach an unrealistic release date—goes away. From the outside looking in, a good Scrum team can seem almost machine-like—they crank out work predictably, iteration after iteration, essentially forever.

WEEK 5

What enterprises must remember is that this lack of drama, this dependability is exactly the type of behavior that should be rewarded. Heroics are only great when they work, and too often when this kind of approach fails, it does so spectacularly. Even when the approach is successful, it can come at a terrible price, with whole teams experiencing burn-out and leaving the program or even the company at the first opportunity. It is important to remember that agile teams are not, in fact, machines. They need to be rewarded and appreciated for the consistent approach to work that they provide. And they need to have opportunities to pursue other kinds of work outside the structure of the iteration that allow them to continue to grow as professionals and individuals.

Part Three

The Agile Path

When you begin to internalize agile values, it changes the way you think and behave at a fundamental level. You learn to function well with limited time, to make commitments with care, and to see that every process, no matter how entrenched, can be changed. Agile practitioners who move beyond a single Scrum role to becoming an agile advocate often take on a visionary role in their organizations. It becomes their job to see what is possible and translate it to the rest of the organization.

Having been an agile coach for many years, I have a great deal of experience coming into organizations and quickly assessing problems. Often, those mired in the problem cannot see it. I, as an outsider, will sometimes spend only a few minutes with a team, and their issues will become obvious to me. To them, however, these problems are merely standard operating procedure. Many times, they literally don't realize there is another way to work.

I believe everyone has infinite capacity for change but not in the same length of time. Change is easier for some people than others. It can be frustrating when you have made the mental leap to agility if those around you have not. Agile advocates and other early adopters in agile practices must take care to not let themselves get mentally beaten down. Being the lone (or nearly lone) voice of agility in an organization can be hard.

But don't get discouraged. Sometimes you have no idea how much you are helping and influencing others. Years ago, I worked as a ScrumMaster on a project that I would consider a failure, and I said as much to a development manager in the organization. "Oh, but you've helped us so much! We would have never accomplished as much on this project without Scrum." I realized that just because my goals for them (a complete move to agility) were not met, it didn't mean they didn't get any benefit. So be patient. Help your organization see the possibilities. They are lucky to have you as a guide and teacher.

Resources

The New New Product Development Game
Takeuchi, Hirotaka and Ikujiro Nonaka. 1986. "The New New Product Development Game." *Harvard Business Review* 33 (1): 1-11. http://en.wikipedia.org/wiki/Scrum_(development)

The Agile Manifesto Website
Beck, Kent et al. 2001. "Manifesto for Agile Software Development." *Agile Manifesto.* http://agilemanifesto.org/

ScrumAlliance: Scrum Is an Innovative Approach to Getting Work Done
"Scrum Is an Innovative Approach to Getting Work Done." *The Scrum Alliance.* http://www.scrumalliance.org/learn_about_scrum

Agile Software Development with Scrum
Schwaber, Ken, and Mike Beedle. 2002. *Agile Software Development with Scrum.* Upper Saddle River: Prentice Hall.

CollabNet White Paper
Druckman, Angela. *Agile Transformation Strategy.* 2011.

Tao Te Ching
Mitchell, Stephen. 1988. *Tao Te Ching.* New York: Harper & Row.

Author's Note - The burndown charts illustrated in this book are simplified versions of those available in ScrumWorks Pro, an agile project management tool created by CollabNet. You can learn more about the features and functionality available in ScrumWorks Pro by visiting the CollabNet website at www.collab.net

Index

A

acceptance criteria, 26, 27, 87, 102, 118
    The Accused, 117–118
    Bait and Switch, 113–115
    Mind Reader, 103–104
    Motherhood and Apple Pie, 104–106
    Needle in a Haystack, 106–107
    of user stories, 134, 138, 157
The Accused, 117–118
action plan, creating, 6, 195
active facilitation technique, 125
agile. *See also* empirical approach;
  Scrum; teams
    approach / framework / principles /
     values,1, 2, 3, 7, 11, 12, 16, 18, 33,
     181, 186, 187, 193, 201, 209
    discipline of, 8–9
    guidelines, 17
    implementation, 4, 204
    iterations, 8, 150, 211–212
    managers, 18
    methods, example, 13
    origins and history, 18–20
    popularity of, 189
    problems, 4–5, 6, 35
    toolkit, 208–209
agile advocates, 213–214
Agile Dirty Dozen red flags, 204–211
Agile Manifesto, 20
Agile Process Mentor, 2

agile product development, definition,
  7–8
agile project management guidelines and
  methods, 17–18, 199
agile transformation, 4, 78, 194, 195–196,
  197, 198, 201–202
Air-brushed Beauty, 182–184
Alternate Universe, 186–189

B

backlog. *See* product backlog
Bad Apples, 43–45, 50
Bait and Switch PBI, 113–115
Big Bang, 190–191
Big Brother combined Scrum role, 73–74
Blob tasks, 108–109
Blue Screen of Death, 134–136
Body Double, 138–140
Boston Marathon example, 84
Brainstormer problem, 70–72
brainstorming sessions, 97
"bug" backlogs, 100, 101
Bully problem, 48–50
burndown and burndown charts, 29. *See
  also* Sprint burndown
    individual and team, 180–181
    release, 184–186
business objectives / goals, 81, 86, 87. *See
  also* goals

business requirements documents (BRDs), 106

C

call-center management, 62, 114
Certified Scrum Master (CSM), 2
Certified Scrum Product Owner (CSPO), 2
Certified Scrum Trainer (CST), 2
change course as implementation phase, 202–204
Cherry Pickers, 166-168
class system teams, 45–47
coach and coaching, 4, 54, 59, 77, 88, 93, 125, 146, 155, 164, 172, 198, 213
commitment, 149, 150, 206–207. *See also* sprint commitment
communication
    breakdown, 10–11
    plan, 53
    on sprint retrospective, 142
    techniques, 125–126
Complainer's Forum, 144–147
complex projects. *See* projects, complex
coordination phase, 197–199, 202
Crystal, 20
culture of fear, 164–165
customer service representatives, 62

D

daily Scrum, 27–28, 27, 28, 31, 112, 119, 120, 128
    Dabbler, 132–133
    DMV, 130–131
    Masquerade, 128–130
Disappearing Act, 52–54
Disguised Waterfall backlog, 93–97
"done / doing / doneness," 66, 69, 79, 102, 107, 111–112, 113, 133, 134, 139
    The Accused, 117–118
    Bait and Switch, 113, 115
    The Hedge, 115–116
"drag and drop," 85

E

Edison, Thomas, 208
Ego War, 156–157
emerging requirements, definition, 13
empirical approach, 11–14, 16, 192. *See also* agile approach / framework; Scrum
Enabler problem, 59–61
epic, 83, 115. *See also* user story
estimation, 149, 150–152
Eternal Optimists, 162–164
cxploration phase, 197–198, 202
Extension Filers, 123–125, 126
eXtreme Programming, 20, 196–197

F

Feature-Driven Development, 20
feedback. *See* sprint review
Fibonacci scale, 153, 160, 172
52-card Pick Up, 121–123
Fire Hose, 191–194
as flexible approach, 13. *See also* agile methods
Foot Draggers, 153–155

G

goals, business, 56, 81, 86, 87. *See also* business objectives
"gold-plating," 110
grooming session, 83, 84, 87, 91, 122, 136, 203

H

The Hedge, 115–116
"The Homework," 4
Hostile Takeover, 136–138

I

Iceberg, 157–159
impediments, and removing, 4, 35–36, 56, 59, 69, 109, 111, 112, 144, 147, 173, 197

inner circle. *See* Scrum inner circle
The Inquisition, 140–142
inspect-and-adapt. *See* Scrum
Instruction Manual user story, 85–87

J

Juggler, 57–59

K

Kitchen Sink user story, 83–85, 95

L

Laundry List backlogs, 98–100
leader/leadership
    Brainstormer as, 70
    command-and-control approach, 16
learning styles, 127

M

Magic Box, 169–171
management / manager, 1, 3, 18, 66. *See also* self-management
    Big Brother, 73–74
    Brainstormer, 70–72
    in burndowns, 180
    Politician, 67–68
    Product Owner, 91
    Slave Driver, 68–70
    in sprint commitment, 165, 171–173, 174, 175
    status report, 188
Marching Orders user story, 87–89
marketing manager, 86–87
Master of Disguise, 55–57
Master of the Universe, 76–78
The Microscope, 177–180
Mind Reader, 103–104
Motherhood and Apple Pie, 104–106
Moving Target backlog, 92–93
Multi-Tasking Mess, 125–127

N

Needle in a Haystack, 106–107
new-product development, 8, 10, 18, 19, 97
Nitpicker, 63–64
Nonaka, Ikujiro, 18, 19

O

"Observations and Recommendations," 4
organization and organizational approaches, 16, 18, 19, 25

P

Perpetual Pessimists, 164–166
"pigs and chickens," 26
planning and planning meetings, 149, 203. *See also* sprint-planning meetings
Pleaders, 49
Poker Tournament, 142–144
Politician, 67–68
PowerPoint in sprint-review meetings, 138–139
predictive approach, 12–16, 150. *See also* waterfall approach
Pressure Cooker, 174–176
prioritization / priorities, of 82, 90, 167. *See also* product backlog, prioritizing
problems, diagnosing, 35–37
process-definition stage, 199–200, 202
product backlog / product backlog item (PBI), 26, 28, 29, 30, 32, 50, 51, 52, 72, 79, 81, 203. *See also* user stories
    acceptance criteria / "done," 102, 113–118
    creating items, 80–82
    organizing, 96, 97
    prioritizing, 89, 92, 101, 188, 190
    purpose, 101
product development, agile, 7, 8. *See also* new-product development

Product Owner, 1, 3, 22, 23, 24–25, 26, 27, 28, 29, 30, 32, 93, 203, 208
   and acceptance criteria, 102, 105, 106, 117–118
   backlog priorities, determining and maintaining, 89, 96, 100–101, 166–117
   in daily Scrum, 128, 133
   and doneness determination, 113, 114–118
   planning, long-term, 161, 184
   releases, 192
   roles, 204–205, 211
   and ScrumMaster, 55, 56, 59, 60, 61
   and sprint commitment, 159, 163, 164, 165, 166, 168–176
   in sprint-planning meeting, 121–121
   and sprint review and retrospective, 133–135, 138–140, 141
   and stakeholders, 62–66, 135, 187
   technical, 85, 87
   and user story doneness, 116–117
project(s)
   complex, 16
   goal, 12, 13, 14, 15, 16
   plan, 11
   reporting, 149, 188
project managers, 24, 55, 58. *See also* ScrumMasters
project-management approaches
   agile, 8, 17–18, 186, 197, 199
   empirical / agile, 11, 20
   guidelines to determine, 17
   Scrum / sprint, 2, 35, 59. 176–177
   traditional / "waterfall," 8, 9–11, 12, 87, 189

Q

quality assurance (QA) in organization, 11
Quota Fillers, 180–182

R

relative estimation, 149–152, 159, 190
   Ego War, 156–157
   Foot Draggers, 153–155
   Iceberg, 157–159
releases, 190–193
release burndown, 184–187, 188
requirements, and requirements document, 11–12, 13, 14, 15–16, 26–27, 79, 122, 170, 186, 189, 203
risk / risk control / risk management, 7, 16, 18, 191
Rock Star, 44–45, 50
rugby metaphor, 19

S

salespeople example, 65
Screamer's List backlog, 90–91
Scrum. *See also* daily Scrum; sprint
   as agile framework / approach, 1, 2, 3, 4, 19, 20–22, 36–37, 187, 196, 197
   artifacts, 29–33
   benefits of, 88, 169, 173
   client tradeoffs with, 189
   derivation of term, 19
   and diagnosing problems, 36
   estimation in, 150
   inspect-and-adapt points, 26 191, 208
   language and mechanics of, 5
   as "management wrapper," 29
   as a pathway, 33
   principles, 181
   product backlog, 30, 203
   roles / goals, 21–22, 166
   and rugby metaphor, 19
   week 1 roles, 39–40
Scrum inner circle, 78, 134, 140, 142, 166, 173, 180, 183, 193, 200, 203, 205
ScrumMasters, 3, 23, 24–25, 26, 27, 61, 173, 209
   and acceptance criteria modeling, 105

ScrumMasters (cont'd)
    and Big Brother combined, 73–74
    and commitments, 165–166
    in daily Scrum, 128–130, 131, 133, 133
    and relative estimation, 154–155, 157
    roles, 1, 3, 39–41, 54–57, 76, 77–78,
      125, 128–130, 133, 205
    in sprint-planning meetings, 126–127
    in sprint retrospective, 141–142, 144–
      145, 147
    in sprint review, 135, 137, 140
    and stakeholders, 110
    and Superman combined, 74–76
Scrum meetings, 119–120. *See also* sprint-
  planning meetings
Scrum roles, combining, 72–73
    Big Brother, 73–74
    Master of the Universe, 76–77
    Superman, 74–75
Scrum team, 22, 23, 25, 26–31, 33, 101,
  174, 192, 200, 201, 205, 211. *See also*
  teams
    and acceptance criteria, 138–140
    burndowns, 181
    cherry-picking, 166–1689
    commitment, 159–161, 162–164,
      181, 182, 183, 206
    communication in, 143, 144
    releases, 193
    in sprint retrospective, 145, 147
    and sprint review, 133–134
    and story points, 171
Secret Agenda tasks, 109–110
self-management, 41–43, 47, 68, 73, 74,
  173, 183, 186, 204, 210
Self-Serve Buffet, 100–101
sheep, in Scrum, 40-43, 69
"shelfware," 14
Slave Driver, 68–70
software development
    agile approach to, 7, 8, 10, 12
    early / iterative, 19
    waterfall approach to, 11

sprint
    backlog, 29, 30–32
    Eternal Optimists, 162–164
    Perpetual Pessimists, 164–166
    Product Owner's 168–169
    and relative estimation, 150, 153, 155,
      158
    Scrum team perspective, 159–161
    stakeholders', 168–169
    story points and, 161
    teams, 23, 30
sprint burndown and burndown chart, 29,
  31–33, 149, 177–180, 182
sprint commitment, 23, 30, 107, 109, 110,
  121, 122, 123, 124, 125, 127, 140, 176
    owner's and stakeholders'
      perspective, 168–176
    project management, 176–177
    scrum team, 159–168, 181
    and sprint burndown charts, 178, 180
sprint management, 176–178
sprint-planning meetings, 1, 26–27, 30,
  48, 52, 60, 84, 96, 98, 101, 118, 203,
  209
    and acceptance criteria, 138
    52-card Pick Up, 121–123
    Multi-Tasking Mess, 125–127
    week 3, 119–121, 126
sprint retrospective, 28–29, 119, 120
    Complainer's Forum, 144–147
    feedback in, 141
    Inquisition, 140–142
    Poker Tournament, 142–144
    purpose, 140
    trust in, 142–143
sprint review, 28, 113, 115, 119, 120,
  133–134
    Blue Screen of Death, 134–136
    Body Double, 138–140
    Hostile Takeover, 136–138
    purposes of, 133–134
    stakeholders and, 134–137

squeaky rats, 132
stakeholders, 22, 26, 28, 98, 187, 190, 203, 206. *See also* Management
  and burndowns, 178–180
  feedback from 136–137, 191
  interference by, 109–110
  and Product Owner, 72
  in relative estimation, 158
  roles, 39–42, 51, 61, 62–66, 80, 113, 122, 134, 135, 141, 187
  sprint commitment, 168–176
  in sprint retrospective, 141–142
  in sprint review, 134–135, 136–137, 140
Starvation Diet backlog, 96–98
story points, 160–161, 171–172, 174, 189
Story-Time / Story-Time meetings, 29, 84, 102, 117, 122, 123, 137, 190
strategic alignment stage, 200–201, 202
Superman (Scrum combined), 74–75
Sustainable pace, 176
system
  complexity, graph, 14–15
  maintenance, 9

T

Takeuchi, Hirotaka, 18, 19
Tao Te Ching, 69
task(s)
  adding, 107
  boards, 109
  Blob, 108–109
  list, 158
  Secret Agenda, 109–110
Task Purgatory, 111–112
teams, agile, 18–19, 20, 22, 23, 27–29, 31, 33, 55–56, 165–166. *See also* Scrum teams
  burnout, 212
  cherry-picking, 166–167
  Class system, 45–47
  in daily Scrum, 129–130, 131, 132–133

teams, agile (cont'd)
  defining tasks, 107
  and doneness, 115
  Ego War, 156–157
  impediments, 111
  manager , 48
  pessimistic, 164
  and relative estimation, 152, 153–155, 157, 158
  roles 1, 40–43
  self-managed, 47, 56, 172, 183
  in sprint-planning meetings, 121, 127, 133
  in sprint retrospective, 146
  in sprint review, 135, 136
  trust, 140–143
technical debt and technical death, 175–176
technological risk and complexity / technical professionals, 14, 18, 111, 156, 167, 169
timebox / time-boxing, 7, 8, 10, 150, 173, 207
time considerations, 5–6
tradeoffs, 186, 188, 189, 210–211
transformation stage, 201–202. *See also* agile
trust, 209
  within teams, 140–143, 172, 181

U

uncertainty (and graph), 14–15, 16, 18
user stories, 79, 80–82, 95, 96, 113, 125, 187, 203
  and acceptance criteria, 102, 105, 106, 107, 114, 138
  composition, 82
  doneness determination, 113–118
  and Fibonacci scale, 160–161
  prioritization of, 89
  relative estimation of, 151, 152, 154, 157, 158, 159, 160

user stories (cont'd)
    in release, 190
    and sprint review, 133–134
    stakeholders, 97
    teams using, 171
    template, 81
Usurper, 65–66

V

velocity and velocity metric, 172, 174,
    175, 176

W

waterfall approach, 8, 9–11, 14, 122,
    150, 166–167, 190. *See also* predictive
    approach
Wimp, 50–52
Wish-lister (stakeholder), 62–63

Y

Yoga, studio example of backlog, 94